Ernest Alexander Cruikshank

The Origin and Official History of the Thirteenth Battalion of

Infantry

A Description of the Work of the Early Militia of the Niagara Peninsula in the War

of 1812 and the Rebellion of 1837

Ernest Alexander Cruikshank

The Origin and Official History of the Thirteenth Battalion of Infantry
A Description of the Work of the Early Militia of the Niagara Peninsula in the War of 1812 and the Rebellion of 1837

ISBN/EAN: 9783743442009

Manufactured in Europe, USA, Canada, Australia, Japa

Cover: Foto ©ninafisch / pixelio.de

Manufactured and distributed by brebook publishing software
(www.brebook.com)

Ernest Alexander Cruikshank

The Origin and Official History of the Thirteenth Battalion of

Infantry

THE

ORIGIN AND OFFICIAL HISTORY

OF THE

THIRTEENTH BATTALION

OF INFANTRY

AND

A DESCRIPTION OF THE WORK OF THE EARLY MILITIA OF
THE NIAGARA PENINSULA IN THE WAR OF 1812
AND THE REBELLION OF 1837

BY

LIEUTENANT-COLONEL E. A. CRUIKSHANK

COMMANDING 44TH BATTALION

E. L. RUDDY

HAMILTON

1899

From the First Settlement to the War of 1812

In A PROVINCE that has been largely settled from first to last by soldiers and the sons of soldiers, it is but natural that a militia force should have been formed spontaneously and almost without an effort on the part of the Government, and too often, it must be added, with scant encouragement on its part.

As early as the summer of 1782 a few discharged soldiers from Lieut.-Colonel John Butler's corps of Rangers began a settlement on the west bank of the River Niagara, near the site of the present town of that name. Next year they were joined by others, and in 1784 the entire regiment was disbanded and officers and men were assigned lands in the twenty townships which were shortly afterwards surveyed for the purpose on the Niagara Peninsula, and composed the original County of Lincoln, bounded to westward by the tract of land along the Grand River, granted to the Indians of the Six Nations. The two battalions of the King's Royal Regiment of New York, the King's Rangers, the Loyal Rangers and fragments of other American loyalist corps, with some men from regular British and German regiments, forming a body of nearly four thousand men were at the same time similarly settled on Crown lands bordering on the Bay of Quinte and River St. Lawrence.

That these men were excellent soldiers there can be no question. Major Potts, of the 8th or King's Regiment, who had been appointed to inspect Butler's Rangers before their disbandment reported that "two thirds of the privates were as fine fellows as he ever saw collected together." These men were inured to every hardship. By their enemies they were naturally hated and accused of being cruel and merciless, for they had carried fire and sword for seven years with tireless energy along the border of the revolting provinces, from Vermont to Kentucky, and the flower of the American frontiersmen had gone down before their onset at Oraskany, Wyoming, Minniesink, Sandusky, the Blue Licks and many another desperate encounter in the forest, from which few of the defeated party had escaped to tell the story of their disaster.

Of these men and their sons the first militia regiments of the province were formed.

The first official enrollment of the militia was accomplished in 1788 and showed an aggregate of 1,525 of all ranks in the district of Lunenburg, 1,141 in Mecklenburg, 600 in Nassau or Niagara, and 721 French-Canadian and 226 British in Hesse or Detroit.

At its second session in 1793, the Legislature of the newly formed Province of Upper Canada passed a Militia Act. All militiamen were thereby required to provide themselves not only with suitable clothing but with arms, accoutrements and a stated quantity of ammunition. But Lieut.-Governor Simcoe recommended that a request from the MacDonnells of Glengarry to be supplied with broadswords from the Government store should be granted, and that muskets should be provided for the whole of the militia. By amendments to this act the next year militiamen were rendered liable to service in manning vessels on the lakes.

A considerable quantity of arms was distributed, and as war with the United States for some time seemed almost inevitable, the militia of the province was formally enrolled and organized into companies and regiments. On the 17th of February, 1794, Lord Dorchester, the Governor-General of Canada, after referring to General Wayne's projected movement upon Detroit, instructed Lieut.-Governor Simcoe to take steps towards occupying the most advantageous positions with a view to resisting Gen. Wayne's attack should he attempt by force to take possession of the country.

Simcoe proceeded to carry out these instructions by forming a military post at the rapids of the Miami and another on an island in the mouth of that river. Two hundred militia were called out for the defence of Detroit and double that number were embodied in the Niagara settlement, which he termed

Major-General E. T. H. Hutton, C.B., A.D.C. to the Queen
commanding the militia of canada

" the bulwark of Upper Canada." The treaty concluded by Mr. Jay put an end to this period of alarm, but efforts continued to be made to improve the organization of the militia, as it was decided to withdraw all the regiments of the regular army then stationed in Upper Canada, for they were sorely needed elsewhere. In 1796 a second battalion of the Royal Canadian Volunteer Regiment of Foot, consisting of nine companies, was enlisted in the province and the command was given to that gallant officer, Lieut.-Colonel John MacDonnell, late of the 84th Regiment. It was distinctly a local corps, and for the next six years, in conjunction with the Queen's Rangers, formed the sole garrison of the province.

An official return of the enrolled militia for the year 1805 shows an aggregate of 652 officers and 7,047 non-commissioned officers and privates. Of the whole number only 200 had received any military training for several years. The unsatisfactory state of relations between Great Britain and the United States had then again begun to excite alarm. As the regular force in the province did not exceed 400 men, the militia were once more ordered to hold themselves in readiness for service and about 4,000 stands of arms were distributed among them. A comprehensive militia act was framed and passed into law providing for a much better organization than any former act, and enabling the Governor to march the militia out of the province to the assistance of the province of Lower Canada when actually invaded or in a state of insurrection, or in pursuit of " an enemy who may have invaded this province and also for the destruction of any vessel or vessels built or building, or any depot or magazine formed or forming, or for the attack of any enemy who may be embodying or marching for the purpose of invading this province, or for the attack of any fortification now erected or which may be hereafter erected to cover the invasion thereof." Lieut.-Governor Gore was evidently very well satisfied with this act, but General Brock indicated the weak point in the act by the remark that it contained " many wise and salutary provisions but few means of enforcing them."

Meanwhile the population continued to increase rapidly, chiefly, however, by the arrival of emigrants from the United States, many of them with strong revolutionary proclivities which they were little inclined to conceal. These men settled in great numbers in the Western, London, Home and Newcastle Districts, where they formed centres of disaffection, and began to plot the overthrow of the Government and the annexation of the province to the United States. Their representations unquestionably led the American Government to believe that the country could be practically conquered by a proclamation calling upon the people to rise and join a small invading army.

Chapter II

A SURVEY of the military strength of the Province of Upper Canada, dated December 2nd, 1811, General Brock assured the Governor-General that "although perfectly aware of the number of improper characters who have obtained extensive possessions and whose principles diffuse a spirit of insubordination very adverse to all military institutions, I still feel confident a large majority will prove faithful. It is, however, certain," he added, "that the the best policy to be pursued, should future circumstances call for active preparations, will be to act with the utmost liberality, and as if no mistrust existed. For unless the inhabitants give an active and efficient aid it will be utterly impossible for the very limited number of the military who are likely to be employed, to preserve the Province." The militia available for the defence of the Detroit frontier numbered only about 700, and the garrison of Fort Amherstburg consisted of but 100 regulars. About 3,000 militia and perhaps 500 Indians, he believed, could be assembled in an emergency on the Niagara River, but he qualified this estimate by the statement that "unless a strong military force be present to animate the loyal and control the disaffected, nothing effectual can be expected." The total number of persons actually liable to perform militia service in the entire Province was estimated at 11,000, of whom the Governor-General considered that it would not be prudent to arm more than 4,000.

One of the first measures undertaken by the Government in anticipation of hostilities was to authorize the formation of a battalion of 400 rank and file among the Highland emigrants, to be known as the Glengarry Light Infantry. Within six weeks from the time that enlisting orders were received it was recruited up to its full strength and their establishment was soon after increased to 600, which was completed before the end of the year. The regiment was sent to the front and took a distinguished part in many actions. In several of the engagements they lost heavily.

By General Brock's advice two companies were selected from each regiment of militia to be trained as flank companies, by which means it was estimated that a force of about 1,800 men would be produced in the whole Province. The Militia Act was amended for this purpose in March, 1812, and the sum of £5,000 voted by the Legislature to enable it to be carried into effect. Some flank companies were immediately organized in the most populous counties, and as both officers and men were required to serve without pay, and many of them were obliged to travel a great distance to attend parade, Brock recommended that authority might at least be granted him to issue rations and provide them with clothing at the expense of the Government. By the 15th of May, 1812, he was able to report, after making a tour of inspection through the County of Lincoln that " the flank companies in the districts in which they have been established were instantly completed with volunteers and, indeed, an almost unanimous disposition to serve is daily manifested. I shall proceed to extend this system, now that I have ascertained that the people are so well disposed, but my means are very limited."

As soon as the declaration of war became known the flank companies of Lincoln militia, numbering about 800 men, were assembled on the Niagara River. They turned out " very cheerfully," but, as they were absolutely unprovided with haversacks, blankets, kettles or tents, they were exposed to extreme discomfort, and soon began to exhibit signs of impatience. Yet it was absolutely impossible to provide them with camp equipage of any kind until it could be forwarded from Montreal or Quebec. A general order of July 4th, 1812, announces that General Brock " has witnessed with the highest satisfaction the orderly and regular conduct of such of the militia as have been called into actual service, and their evident desire to acquire military instruction. He is sensible that they are exposed to great privations and every effort will be immediately made to supply their most pressing wants, but such are the circumstances of the country that it is absolutely necessary that every inhabitant should have recourse to his own means to furnish himself with blankets and other necessaries."

Similar bodies were at the same time collected at Cornwall, Prescott, Kingston, Amherstburg and Sandwich. It was at the last named point that the first invasion of the Province took place on the 12th of July, 1812, and for some weeks the militia of Essex and Kent, intimidated by the numbers and threats of the enemy, and influenced by the evil example of some of their officers, behaved badly, deserting to their homes in numbers and refusing to return to duty. Within a few days after the appearance of an invading army on British soil, a blow was struck in the west which was destined to have the most important results. Captain Roberts, who commanded a party of invalid soldiers at the island of St. Joseph, succeeded without difficulty in organizing a small

LIEUTENANT-COLONEL W. D. OTTER, A. D. C.,
COMMANDING MILITARY DISTRICT No. 2.

battalion of volunteers among the boatmen and other employees of the fur companies, at the head of whom and his regulars he moved against the American fort of Mackinac and took it, without even a show of resistance. He attributed his easy success largely to "the unparallelled exertions of the Canadians who had manned his boats and dragged his artillery into a commanding position."

General Brock promptly determined to assail the invading force at Sandwich, before it could receive support, and with 400 picked men assembled at Port Dover and transported them in row boats to Amherstburg. On arriving there it was learned that the enemy had retired across the river. General Brock resolved to follow, and he landed in Michigan on the morning of the 16th of August with 1,330 men, of whom 400 were militia selected from the flank companies of the Essex, Kent, Oxford, Norfolk, Lincoln and York regiments. The surrender of the American force with the town and fort of Detroit took place the same day.

The subsequent good conduct of the Essex and Kent militia amply atoned for any misconduct in the beginning of the war. In September a detachment from the two Essex regiments accompanied Major Muir's expedition against Fort Wayne and it is stated to have behaved remarkably well. A month later another under Lieut. Dewar occupied an advanced position at the Miami Rapids. During the following winter detachments performed garrison duty at Amherstburg, Detroit and even Mackinac. Twelve officers and 104 men of the 1st Essex and nine officers and 87 men of the 2nd Essex, under Major Robert Reynolds, were engaged in the battle at the River Raisin, January 22nd, 1813. Five privates were killed and sixteen men were wounded.

Thirty-four officers and 482 men took part in the expedition against Fort Meigs on the Miami River, April 23rd to May 9th 1813; Captain Bondy of the 1st Essex was killed in action and four privates wounded.

After the withdrawal of the British regular forces from this frontier in October, 1813, a company commanded by Lieut. James McGregor, known as the Loyal Kent Volunteers, performed some notable service. In December Lieut. McGregor with seven of his men joined Lieut. Medcalf of the Norfolk militia in an attack on an American post at McRae's house, below Chatham, in which the whole of the enemy's party was captured. In January, 1814, he crossed the River St. Clair into Michigan, and brought off as a prisoner an American captain of militia, together with the arms of his company which were stored in his house. About a month later he received instructions to cover the passage of the river by 200 Indians who were conveying arms and ammunition to the western tribes, a service which was successfully performed. But on the 4th of March the Loyal Kent Volunteers and a company of Essex Rangers, lately raised by Captain William Caldwell of Amherstburg, supported by eight com-

LIEUTENANT-COLONEL HENRY McLAREN,
COMMANDING THIRTEENTH BATTALION OF INFANTRY.

panies of the Royal Scots and 89th Regiment, attacked a body of 160 American riflemen who had entrenched themselves on the bank of the Fourteen Mile Creek near Delaware, but were repulsed with severe loss. In this action Lieut. McGregor was badly wounded, as were also a sergeant and five privates of his company.

For some time after the surrender of Detroit, the flank companies of the Norfolk regiments were excused from service, but in November, 1812, four companies, commanded by Captains John Bostwick, Abram Rapelje, Daniel McCall and Lieut. Brewster Brigham, were ordered to Fort Erie. On the morning of the 28th of November, being stationed at the ferry opposite Black Rock and hearing musketry on the bank of the river below, Bostwick's and Rapelje's companies hastened to the point of attack. They soon became closely engaged with a body of the enemy that had landed and carried two small batteries, but finding themselves outnumbered and the enemy in possession of the artillery, were obliged to retreat with considerable loss.

October, 1813, brought a signal reverse on the Thames. The Niagara Peninsula was, in consequence, practically abandoned, and the remnant of General Proctor's defeated brigade fell back on Burlington, which for some weeks was the most advanced post occupied by the British forces. The militia had been disbanded and parties of marauders over-ran the country from which the troops had retired. One of these, composed largely of refugees from Canada, advancing from Buffalo, appeared in the township of Woodhouse early in November. On the 13th Lieut.-Colonel Henry Bostwick went in pursuit of them with forty-five volunteers, formed in two companies under Captains John Bostwick and Daniel McCall. The house in which the marauders had taken post was quietly surrounded. Captain Bostwick, accompanied by Lieut. Austin, advanced to demand their surrender, but on entering the building he was surprised to find it crowded with men who sprang to arms, and observing that he was apparently unsupported, fired two shots at him, inflicting a slight wound, and made him a prisoner. On hearing the report of firearms in the house the remainder of the militia rushed forward and were fired at by the enemy from the windows. The fire was at once returned and some of the enemy ran out and attempted to escape, but were shot down or taken. The rest then surrendered. Three had been killed, several were badly wounded and eighteen taken prisoners.

It is not surprising that as the County of Lincoln, as it was then constituted, formed the principal seat of war, its militia should be called to arms more frequently than any other in the actual defence of their homes. The population of the county was estimated to exceed 12,000, and the militia, organized into six battalions, numbered nearly 2,400 of all ranks. The line of defence along the Niagara River was organized in July, 1812, into four divisions, each composed of a section of field artillery, a detachment of the 41st Regiment and a body of militia.

On the 10th of July one-half of the militia were allowed to return home on furlough, as there appeared to be no immediate danger of an attack, the preference being given to "those whose presence on the farms are most required to bring in the harvest." But on the 22nd, when particulars of the invasion of the province at Sandwich became known, all militiamen absent on furlough were ordered to rejoin their regiments. Five hundred men were soon afterwards ordered to hold themselves in readiness to join the flank companies on the frontier at a moment's notice. After the surrender of Detroit, the conclusion of an armistice afforded General Brock an opportunity of permitting four-fifths of each flank company to return home for a few days.

Notice of the termination of the armistice was received on the 4th of September, and the flank companies of the Lincoln regiments were not only recalled but those of the three York regiments were brought over to Fort George. The first casualty occurred on the 19th of September, when Private John Hendershot of the 1st Lincoln, while on sentry duty at the Lime-kilns near Queenstown, was killed by a shot from the American bank.

In a very gallant attempt to recover the brig Detroit from the enemy in the river above Squaw Island, on the 9th of October, Major Pell, of the Niagara Dragoons was mortally wounded.

On the 5th of November one-tenth of the militia companies sta-

LIEUTENANT-COLONEL THE HON. ISAAC BUCHANAN,
COMMANDING 13TH BATT., 1862-1865.

tioned at Fort George and Chippawa were attached to Captain Powell's company of artillery, to be trained in the use of garrison and field guns.

In announcing the termination of the armistice in a general order of the 20th of November, General Sheaffe contented himself with saying :

"To men who have already so nobly conducted themselves before the enemy, it would be superfluous in the Major-General to say more than that he is persuaded that whenever the opportunity shall present itself they will again prove themselves worthy of the glorious cause in which they are engaged, and successfully defend their country, their families and property."

On the morning of the 28th of November when it became known that the enemy had effected a landing below Fort Erie in considerable force, Captain James Kerby of the Lincoln Artillery, with a field gun, marched from Chippewa with Captain Hamilton's company of the 2nd Lincoln and a small party of the 41st Regiment. After passing Block Creek they overtook Major Hatt with detachments of his own and other Lincoln regiments numbering about 200 men. On arriving at Frenchman's Creek they encountered the rear-guard of the invaders, consisting of thirty-eight men, commanded by Captain King, aide-de-camp to General Smyth. They succeeded in taking them prisoners without loss. Eighteen boats full of men were then discovered crossing the river, which were driven back by the fire of the field piece and a few rounds of musketry. Two of the boats were sunk and about 30 men killed and wounded in this attack. Major Hatt, Captain Kerby and Lieuts. Bryson and Ball of the Lincoln Artillery were specially mentioned in the dispatches.

An order of the 7th of December announced that a cessation of active operations might soon be expected.

One week afterwards the flank companies of the 2nd and 3rd York and the battalion companies of the Lincoln regiments were released from duty. The Lincoln flank companies were retained in service until the end of the year.

Their duties during the months of November and December were extremely arduous and exhausting.

A serious alarm occurred early in February, 1813, as a considerable division of American regular troops was assembled near Buffalo, and Lake Erie was firmly frozen over.

"There being some reason to believe that the enemy meditates some attempt on the frontiers" the Adjutant-General of Militia wrote to Lieut.-Colonel Clark of the 2nd Lincoln on the 11th of February, " I am directed to desire that you will with all possible expedition assemble not only the flank companies but as many spirited young men in addition as can be induced to join them at Chippewa, where quarters will be prepared for their reception.

" His Honor, the Major-General Sheaffe, trusts that on this occasion both the officers and men will recollect the very honorable and successful manner in which they have hitherto contributed to the defence of the province, and that for a little time longer private considerations will give way to public."

Nor was this apprehension ill founded, for the American Secretary of War had actually authorized another attempt at invasion. "As the season has now furnished you with a bridge as well for retreat as advance," he wrote to Colonel Porter, the officer commanding at Buffalo, "it is thought advisable that you do not permit circumstances so favorable to escape without making a stroke on such points of the enemy's line as may be within your reach."

The flank companies of the 2nd and 3rd Lincoln and the two Norfolk regiments were immediately marched to the frontier and stationed along the shore of Lake Erie, from Fort Erie to Sugar Loaf Point. This show of vigilance combined with the desertion of a trusted non-commissioned officer from Buffalo, had the effect of preventing any offensive operation being undertaken beyond the bombardment of Fort Erie by the batteries at Block Rock on the 17th of March. Seventeen hundred militia were actually called out at that time to meet the impending attack, but after a few weeks service the whole, with the exception of a few flank companies, were again disbanded.

A detachment of three officers and sixty-three men taken in equal proportions from the 2nd York, 4th and 5th Lincoln, under Major Simons of the first named regiment, was stationed during April and May at Burlington, to maintain communication between York and Niagara. From this post they were obliged to retire by a superior force of the enemy in two armed schooners, who landed there on the morning of May 10th, under cover of the guns of their vessels, and destroyed a small barracks.

Upon the evacuation of Fort Erie by the regular troops, Major John Warren, of the 3rd Lincoln effectually dismantled the batteries and destroyed the public stores before retiring, while Lieut.-Colonel Clark, of the 2nd Lincoln, performed a similar service at Chippewa and Queenston. The greater part of these regiments was then quietly disbanded, only sixty militiamen in addition to Captain Runchey's company of negroes and Merritt's troop of Provincial Dragoons, having accompanied Vincent's division in its retreat to Burlington. The Americans made great efforts to parole all the inhabitants that had remained at home, and in two weeks had secured a list of five hundred persons who had given their parole in the County of Lincoln.

On the retreat of the invading army from Stoney Creek, the spirit of the loyal militia along their line of march was thoroughly aroused. General Vincent at once advanced, as he stated, "to give encouragement to the militia and yeomanry of the country who are everywhere rising upon the fugitive Americans and making them prisoners, and with-holding all supplies from them." On the 9th of June a party of the 2nd Lincoln captured a depot of provisions formed by the enemy near Queenston and actually took possession of the village itself.

The blockade at the American camp at Fort George was then discontinued. On the 9th of October the British forces retired to Burlington, and for two months the Niagara Peninsula lay open to the incursions of the enemy's irregular troops and marauding parties. The militia were disbanded and mostly disarmed.

During the whole of the campaign Captain W. H. Merritt's troop of Provincial Dragoons had been most actively employed and performed effective service. Major Lisle of the 19th Dragoons, under whose orders they served from July, 1813, until December, 1814, stated that this corps "were at all times of the most essential service from their perfect knowledge of the country and the zeal and bravery they always displayed in its defence."

The battalion of Incorporated Militia authorized by the Act of Legislature had been recruited nearly to its full strength during the summer and autumn of 1813, chiefly with vigorous young men who had already served in the flank companies, with the exception of Captain William Robinson, of the 8th or King's Regiment, who was selected for the command with the local rank of lieutenant-colonel, and the Adjutant, Dennis FitzGerald, a lieutenant on half-pay of the 41st Regiment; all the other combatant officers were taken from the militia, and most of them were natives of the province or had been born in the United States before the Revolution. A detachment of the new corps consisting of five officers and fifty or sixty non-commissioned officers and men had joined the centre division before Fort George in September, 1813, and other detachments were stationed at Cornwall, Kingston and York. During the winter of 1813-14 the whole of the battalion was assembled at York, and drilled into such an admirable state of discipline and efficiency that Sir Gordon Drummond determined to move it forward into the first line of defence on the Niagara, and withdraw one of the regular battalions, but before this was accomplished the enemy had again passed the river and the campaign had actually begun. On the 22nd of June, 1814, the battalion at York mustered twenty-nine officers and 402 non-commissioned officers and men. As soon as the landing of the enemy became known the 2nd Lincoln was assembled at Chippawa nearly three hundred strong. In conjunction with the light companies of the Royal Scots and 100th Regiment and a body of Indians, it formed the advance of the British forces in the hard fought action at Street's Creek on the 5th of July, 1814, when after a warm contest the brigade of General Peter B. Porter, composed of volunteers and Indians from New York and Pennsylvania, was dislodged and routed with considerable loss in killed and wounded, and several of the officers made prisoners; Lieut. Colonel Dickson was badly wounded, and the command devolved on Major David Secord, a veteran of the American Revolution, who continued the action with great bravery and judgment. Captains Rowe and Turney, Ensign Macdonell and nine non-commissioned officers and men were killed; Lieuts. Clement and Bowman, Ensign Kirkpatrick and twelve rank and file wounded, while fifteen others reported as missing were also supposed to have been killed or wounded in the woods where the action took place.

At this time the 1st Brigade of Militia occupied an advanced position extending from the Ten Mile Creek to De Cew's and Street's Mills. "There was a good deal of skirmishing yesterday," General Riall wrote on the 19th, "with the advance of the militia and the enemy's outposts near St. Davids, and they have in consequence burnt that village and several of the neighboring houses. They have also burnt the whole of the houses between Queenston and the Falls.

18

The 2nd Brigade of Militia, under Lieut.-Colonel Hamilton, is at present at the Forty Mile Creek. I am happy to be able to inform you that almost the whole body of militia is in arms and seems actuated by the most determined spirit of hostility to the enemy." An American field officer fully corroborated this statement that "the whole population is against us, not a foraging party but is fired on and not unfrequently returns with missing numbers."

At the Battle of Lundy's Lane the battalion of Incorporated Militia came into contest with the enemy for the first time. In the early part of this action this corps was suddenly attacked in the flank by the 25th United States Infantry which had gained a commanding position on its left under cover of the darkness. The battalion lost heavily, fell into confusion, and was obliged to retire a short distance, when it was rallied and continued the contest with great steadiness. The total loss of the battalion was considerably more than one third of the whole number engaged.

The unusual proportion of wounded men to the number of killed was attributed to the use of buckshot by the enemy at close range, but many of the wounds were consequently very slight. Detachments of the Norfolk, Oxford and Middlesex Regiments and of the Essex and Kent Rangers arrived during the latter part of the battle, but were held in reserve and sustained no loss.

LIEUTENANT-COLONEL ALFRED BOOKER,
COMMANDING 13TH BATT. 1865-1866.

Although much reduced in numbers the battalion of Incorporated Militia shortly afterwards took an active and distinguished part in the investment of Fort Erie.

In a campaign of less than two months, beginning on the 25th of July and ending on the 17th of September, out of twenty-nine officers belonging to the Incorporated Militia three were killed and thirteen wounded, and upwards of one hundred and fifty non-commissioned officers and men were killed or wounded. It was disbanded by a general order dated March 10th, 1815.

19

The militia of the remaining counties of Upper Canada were afforded much less opportunity of earning distinction, but showed no less zeal and alacrity whenever summoned to defend the frontier, and likewise furnished their full quota for the Incorporated Militia. As soon as the declaration of war became known, the flank companies of the Eastern and Johnstown Districts assembled at Cornwall and Prescott and those of the Midland District at Kingston. By July 5th six hundred militia had marched into the latter town and a party of sixty men under Captain Patrick Smith sent in boats to escort some British merchant vessels into port fell in with a fleet of nine American sloops and schooners at the Upper Narrows, two of which they took and burnt and drove the remainder back to Ogdensburg, where they were blocaded for several weeks. Another party at Cornwall, commanded by Captain John Kerr, took a large number of large Durham boats ascending the St. Lawrence, one of which was converted into the gunboat Brock.

For several months during the winter of 1812-13 Ogdensburg was garrisoned by a battalion of United States Rifles under Captain Forsyth, a very enterprising and aggressive officer, who began to annoy the inhabitants of the opposite shore by a succession of petty attacks. As early as January 19th, 1813, Colonel Vincent, then commanding at Kingston, complained to General Dodge, the commandant at Sackett's Harbor, of "the military excursions of Captain Forsyth which can have no other object in view than injury to private individuals and to increase the miseries of war to them without the possibility or even prospect of its attaining any public or private advantage." If they were not discontinued, he said, he would be forced to take such measures in self defence "as may prove very destructive to the villages and settlements on that frontier which is by no means my wish if it can be avoided."

General Dodge appears to have concurred in Vincent's estimate of Forsyth's operations for he replied that he would "take the earliest opportunity to caution the commanding officer at Ogdensburg against that inefficient mode of warfare."

Undeterred by this warning, Forsyth made a descent on Brockville on the morning of February 6th, where he surprised a flank company of the 1st Leeds Militia and made prisoners of Major Carley, Captains Ives and Stuart, Lieut. Morris and about twenty non-commissioned officers and men with nearly an equal number of unarmed inhabitants. There was no public property at the place except the arms of the militia. In reporting this incursion Lieut.-Colonel Sherwood of the Leeds Regiment suggested the propriety of retaliating by an attack on Ogdensburg if his force could be increased, and sent Captain Duncan Fraser with forty-five men across the river to reconnoitre on the night of February 7th. Fraser took a sentry and drove in the pickets when he retired without loss.

Two weeks then elapsed before the necessary permission for the attempt could be obtained. But at sunrise on February 2nd, Major George MacDonnel of the Glengarry Light Infantry, at the head of 210 regular troops and 270 militia under Lieut.-Colonel Thomas Fraser, made a direct frontal attack on the American batteries at that place. They were taken after an obstinate resistance, which cost him over fifty men in killed and wounded.

In the winter of 1813-14 a very successful little enterprise was planned and carried into execution by Captain Reuben Sherwood, of the Leeds Militia. On the 6th of February, 1814, he crossed the river from Point Iroquois to Hamilton with a subaltern and twenty Royal Marines and ten men of the Incorporated Militia, commanded by Captain Kerr. Guards were posted about the village, and every horse and sleigh in the place impressed, and he pushed rapidly forward fourteen miles inland to Madrid (now Columbia Village), where he recovered a large quantity of merchandise captured from British merchants on its way up the St. Lawrence the year before, and returned without molestation next day. " This bold excursion," says Dr. Hough, the local historian, " convinced the people that their lives and property were at the mercy of the British." It was followed up by a much more important raid by a column of about 600 regulars and militia under Colonel Scott, of the 103rd Regiment, also conveyed in sleighs, which destroyed the barrack at French Mills and brought off a great quantity of stores, February 19th to 24th, 1814.

The services of the militia during the contest, therefore, were neither few nor unimportant. The number actually enrolled in Upper and Lower Canada has been stated at 7,286, of whom 186 were cavalry, 163 artillery, 323 voltigeurs and 6,617 infantry. After the lapse of nearly thirty-five years a medal was struck to commemorate the deeds of the British army from 1793 to 1814, and strangely enough the only military operations in Canada considered worthy of notice in this manner were the capture of Detroit, the skirmish at Chateauguay and the battle of Chrysler's Farm. At Detroit and Chateauguay there was practically no fighting worth mentioning, and no militia had been engaged at Chrysler's Farm. The bloodiest and most important battles of the war, Queenston, the River Raisin, Miami, Stoney Creek, and Lundy's Lane, were absolutely unnoticed. Five hundred and thirty-one medals were, however, awarded to militiamen, 267 to residents of Upper Canada and 264 to persons living in Lower Canada ; and clasps were apportioned, 221 for Detroit, 260 for Chateauguay and 55 for Chrysler's Farm. Three militiamen proved their title to two clasps each, and one, Jean Baptist LeClair, to all three, but it is safe to say that the majority of the men who had seen the hardest fighting and performed the best service, received no recognition at this time.

CHAPTER III

THE MILITIA OF 1837-8

THE POPULATION of the province increased more than five fold during the course of the next quarter of a century, but as usual in a time of profound peace the militia force was much neglected, although a nominal organization was maintained and the regiments were still assembled for inspection and what was termed "general training" once a year.

Dissatisfaction with the administration of the affairs of the province had grown pronounced from the conviction that power and patronage was concentrated in the hands of a number of selfish and arbitrary persons who exercised their authority in an arrogant and despotic manner for the aggrandizement of themselves, their relatives and adherents, and had in consequence become odious under the name of the "Family Compact." The prevalence of this feeling gave the opposition a decided majority in the Legislative Assembly at the elections of 1835, but the "Family Compact" still controlled the Legislative Council which was constituted by appointment. The leaders of the popular party, however, soon became involved in a controversy with the new Lieutenant-Governor, Sir Francis Head, who had convinced himself that they were republicans at heart and that independence or annexation to the United States was their ultimate aim. He dissolved the Assembly and issued a manifesto in which he appealed to the loyalty of the inhabitants and denounced his "Radical" opponents as seditious and revolutionary. For some time afterwards the Lieutenant-Governor was kept busy answering "loyal" addresses which poured in upon him from the "Constitutionists" or "Tories." In one of these replies which was printed and widely circulated as a campaign document, he pointedly referred to a letter from Mr. Papineau to Mr. Bidwell, speaker of the Assembly, which had lately been published, calling upon the people of both the Canadas to "unite as a man."

22

Lieutenant-Governor Head declared that :

" The people of Upper Canada detest democracy ; they revere their constitutional charter, and are consequently staunch in allegiance to their King.

" They are perfectly aware that there exists at the Lower Province one or two individuals who inculcate the idea that this province is about to be disturbed by the interference of foreigners, whose power and whose numbers will prove invincible.

" In the name of every regiment of militia in Upper Canada, I publicly promulgate let them come if they dare."

This of course was an obvious reference to some hint of invasion from the United States, which even then must have been talked of.

At the elections which followed, his triumph was complete, and there can be little doubt that it was largely due to his direct and opportune appeal to the ingrained loyalty of the mass of the people, who were willing to condone the misdeeds of the Family Compact, rather than seem to endorse sedition.

The result of this election made the Lieutenant-Governor feel so secure of the loyalty of the inhabitants, that when he was asked by Sir John Colborne how many of the regular troops he could spare for the maintenance of order in Lower Canada, he unhesitatingly replied, " all of them," and even refused to retain two companies as a garrison for the city of Toronto.

LIEUTENANT-COLONEL JAMES A. SKINNER, COMMANDING 13TH BATT. 1866-1886.

The standard of rebellion was raised at Montgomery's tavern on the 4th of December, 1837. The time and place seemed well chosen. A serious rising was known to have taken place near Montreal. All the regular troops had been sent to Lower Canada, and four thousand stands of arms were deposited in the Toronto city hall, only three miles away, over which the Lieutenant-Governor had declined even to set a guard. In the country to the northward, Mackenzie, the leader of the rebellion, had many adherents, and some of his most ardent supporters who were prepared to go any length, assured him that fifteen hundred men were already enrolled and prepared to take up arms. As it was, he never succeeded in assembling more than five hundred wretchedly equipped, and as the result proved, anything but stout-hearted men. This, however, was amply sufficient to throw the city into a state of indescribable alarm and confusion, and had he promptly advanced he might have taken it. But the militia soon assembled and was rapidly reinforced by volunteers from the country.

On the 6th, Colonel Allan McNab, then speaker of the House of Assembly, came in from Hamilton with sixty men from Gore District, whom he had assembled at half an hour's notice. Next morning, having upwards of a thousand well armed men at his command, Head determined to march out against the rebels, whose numbers were steadily diminishing. The chief command was vested in Colonel James FitzGibbon, well known from his services at Beaver Dam and elsewhere in the war of 1812, who was then Acting Adjutant General of Militia. The main body was headed by Colonel Allan McNab, the right wing being commanded by Colonel Samuel Jarvis, and the left by Colonel William Chisholm, assisted by the Honorable Justice McLean, late speaker of the House of Assembly; the two guns by Major Carfrae, of the Militia Artillery. The assistance of two officers and eight artillerymen, the sole representatives of the regular troops left in Toronto, was resolutely declined, as the Lieutenant-Governor had determined that the contest should be decided solely by the Upper Canada militia.

When they came in sight of Montgomery's tavern, Mackenzie's supporters at once dispersed. There was scarcely a show of resistance, and happily little bloodshed.

The militia continued to march into Toronto in great numbers from all quarters.

From Gore, Niagara, Lake Simcoe and various other places brave men, armed as well as unarmed, rushed forward unsolicited, and according to the best reports from 10,000 to 12,000 men simultaneously marched towards the capital to support Lieutenant-Governor Head in maintaining the British constitution for the people of Upper Canada.

As their services were not required, they were directed to return to their homes and disband, and in response to a demand from Sir John Colborne an order was issued authorizing the militia of the Bathurst, Johnstown, Ottawa, and eastern districts, to march out of the province and give their assistance to the government of Lower Canada. Colonel Allan McNab was instructed to advance against Dr. Duncombe, who was reported to have assembled a small party in arms at Scotland, in the township of Burford. At his approach, Duncombe's followers dispersed without firing a shot, and McNab scoured the neighboring country in pursuit of them for several days, making numerous arrests of suspicious characters.

Mackenzie made his way in disguise to the house of a sympathizer, named McAffee, who lived on the bank of the Niagara, within sight of Buffalo, and was ferried across the river, narrowly escaping capture. A committee of thirteen prominent citizens of Buffalo had been formed to aid the revolutionary movement in Canada as early as the 5th of December, before it could possibly have been known that an outbreak had taken place in the upper province, and a mass meeting had been called for the evening of the 11th, the very day that Mackenzie arrived in the city, a fugitive and alone. The meeting is described as one of the largest ever held there, and when Dr. Chapin announced that the leader of the Canadian insurrection was then a guest at his house there was a demonstration of wild enthusiasm. A guard of honor of young men was formed for his protection, and it was announced that he would address a meeting on the following evening. The theatre was crammed to hear him. Mackenzie spoke for two hours with his habitual fluency and vigor of invective. General Thomas Jefferson Sutherland followed him, anouncing their intention of invading Canada at once and calling for volunteers and contributions of arms and supplies. At the time there were many laborers, seaman and dockhands idle in the city and consequently recruits

Lieut.-Colonel The Hon. J. M. Gibson A. D. C.
Commanding 13th Battalion 1886-1895.

promised to be plentiful. Within twenty-four hours a band of armed men were assembled at Whitehaven, on Grand Island, under the leadership of General Rensselaer Van Rensselaer, a profligate son of one of the most respected citizens of the state. Mackenzie joined him there and on the 13th they landed with between twenty-five and fifty followers on Navy Island, then quite uninhabited and densely wooded. A proclamation in the name of the Provisional Government was printed in the form of a handbill, stating that "three hundred acres of the most valuable land in Canada and one hundred dollars in money will be given to each volunteer who may join the Patriot forces on Navy Island." They instantly began to erect huts and to fortify their camp. Within a week the patriot flag, bearing two white stars on a blue ground, was said to be waving over the heads of five hundred well armed men. Contributions of arms and provisions came in from many sources.

As soon as the invasion of Navy Island became known, a considerable body of militia was assembled at Chippawa under Colonel Cameron, and the river carefully patrolled. On the 25th, Colonel McNab came in with 500 volunteers fresh from his his successful expedition against Duncombe, and took over the command. Within a few days his force was swelled to 2,500 by volunteers from all quarters. Among them were a company of negroes and a body of Six Nation Indians, from the Grand River, led by Colonel William Johnson Kerr, who had been one of their officers in the War of 1812.

Among other distinguished volunteers who had joined McNab on his march to Burford, was Andrew Drew, a commander in the Royal Navy on half-pay, who had been settled for some years on a farm near Woodstock. Several other naval officers and a number of seamen having come in, a naval brigade, under Drew's command, was soon formed, and vessels and boats collected with the view of attacking the island.

Mackenzie's forces, however, had not been idle. They had cut a road quite around the island, thrown up formidable-looking entrenchments, and obstructed the approaches on the western front. Their numbers were said to have increased to upwards of one thousand, most of whom a Buffalo newspaper described as ruffians "who would cut any man's throat for a dollar."

A desultory artillery fire was opened on the Canadian shore, by which two or three militiamen were killed or wounded and a few houses damaged.

Drew was engaged in preparing boats for crossing, when late on the afternoon of the 29th, while standing in company with McNab at the look-out post, they saw a small steamer put out from Schlosser and cross over to the island. With their field glasses they could see that she was crowded with men, and thought they could distinguish one or two cannons on deck. "This won't do!" exclaimed McNab, "I say Drew, do you think you can cut that vessel out?" "Oh, yes," Drew replied, "nothing can be easier, but it must be done at night." "Well, then," said McNab, "go and do it!"

Sir Francis Head, who had arrived at Chippawa a few days before, was of course consulted, and readily gave his consent to the enterprise. The steamer they had seen was the Caroline, of Buffalo, which had been specially chartered to carry troops and stores to the island.

She tied up on the east side of Navy Island, where she landed her passengers, and seems to have returned to Schlosser after dark, unseen from the Canadian bank. Drew immediately called for volunteers, simply saying that he

26

"wanted a few fellows with cutlasses who would follow him to the devil." Sixty men were selected from the large number that offered, and about midnight they put off in seven boats.

It was bright moonlight, and when he passed the upper end of Navy Island, he saw that the Caroline lay at Schlosser wharf. He was then in no mood to turn back, and directed his men to row across the river. When his boat came within twenty yards of the steamer, it was hailed by the watch on deck, who demanded the countersign. Drew quietly replied, "I will give it to you when I get on board," and urged his men to pull alongside. He scrambled up the side at the starboard gangway, carrying his cutlass between his teeth, but such was the anxiety of his crew to follow that they impeded each other's movements, the boats swung off, and he remained alone on the Caroline's deck for more than a minute. Brandishing his weapon over their heads, Drew said to the watch, which consisted of three men, "Now I want this vessel, and you had better go ashore at once." They ran across the deck, and Drew supposed they were about to obey, when one of them snatched up a musket and and fired it within a yard of his head. The shot missed, and Drew struck the man down with a savage blow of his cutlass. Another man then snapped a pistol in his face but it missed fire, and

LIEUT.-COLONEL A. H. MOORE
COMMANDING 13TH BATTALION 1895-97.

he was instantly disarmed by a quick cut on the arm, and with his remaining companion was driven ashore. By this time the remainder of the boarding party had reached the deck, and in a very short time gained entire possession of the vessel, driving the crew and passengers on the boat ashore. Drew mounted the paddle box and gave orders to cut her moorings and send her adrift. She was found to be attached to the wharf by chains, and some delay occurred before these orders could be executed. A body of men from a tavern near the wharf assembled apparently with the intention of attempting to retake the vessel, and began firing. Lieut. Elmsley advanced with sixteen men, armed only with cutlasses, and took up a position across the street, where he held this party in check until the chains which secured the Caroline were cut loose. · The steamer was finally towed into the current of the river, where she was set on fire and cast adrift. After passing through the rapids, wrapped in flames, she grounded on a small islet near the brink of Niagara Falls, where she subsequently went to pieces. Besides Lieut. McCormack, several others of Drew's party were slightly wounded, while twelve persons out of thirty-three, said to have been on board the Caroline when attacked, were reported missing. Of these, however, only one, Amos Durfee, a negro, was certainly known to be killed. Drew himself believed that there could not have been more than two killed and four or five wounded.

After the destruction of the Caroline the force under McNab was augmented by the arrival of fresh bodies of militia until it exceeded 5,000. The filibusters were also considerably reinforced and for some days a body of them was encamped on Grand Island. Dissensions, however, soon arose among them, for Van Rensselaer was a drunkard and incompetent to command in many ways. On the 13th of January, 1838, Navy Island was finally evacuated by them, having been in their possession exactly a month. Late in December Brigadier-General Sutherland had been sent by Van Rensselaer to Detroit to create a diversion in his favor by an attack on the Canadian frontier from that quarter. On the 7th of January, 1838, Sutherland arrived in Detroit with 200 men. He found three or four hundred men assembled under General Roberts and assumed the command under the authority given him by Van Rensselaer. It was determined to remove to the island of Bois Blanc, in Canadian waters and thence make an attack on Amherstburg in conjunction with the schooner Ann, a gift from an enthusiastic supporter which they had armed with three pieces of cannon. The landing on Bois Blanc was effected without opposition, and during the night the schooner, commanded by General Theller, passed between the island and the Canadian shore, firing into the town.

Immediate preparations were made for an attack upon Amherstburg under cover of the guns of the Ann. In passing down the river by moonlight to take up her position, the vessel was fired upon by a party of Essex militia, under Lieut.-Colonel Radcliffe, who occupied the town. The man at the helm was either shot or deserted his post, and the schooner drifted towards the Canadian shore, where she ran aground. Some of the militia led by Captain Ironside, and Ensign Baby, waded out in the water, which took them up to their armpits, and boarded her. One of her crew had been killed, and they took eight wounded and twelve unwounded prisoners, including all the officers, three pieces of cannon, and 200 stand of arms. This event greatly dispirited Sutherland, who instantly gave orders for a retreat to Sugar Island in American waters, where he was joined next day by General Handy, who came down the river in the steamer Erie with reinforcements and supplies. The number of men under their command was estimated at 700. In a few days the ice began to flow, provisions were falling short, and Handy summoned the Governor of Michigan to his assistance, requesting him to come to Sugar Island, accompanied by a single staff officer, and go through the form of dispersing his forces.

Early in February, Brigadier-General Donald McLeod and Colonel Vreeland arrived at Detroit with a body of men whom they had enlisted in Ohio. On the the night of February 24th they took possession of Fighting Island, below Sandwich, with two or three hundred followers, but were promptly attacked and driven out next day by a detachment of the 32nd Regiment, with a loss of five men wounded. After evacuating Navy Island, Mackenzie and Van Rensselaer planned a movement upon Kingston, where they seem to have anticipated a rising in their favor. In the prosecution of this enterprise the United States Arsenal at Watertown, N. Y. was broken into and robbed of a large quantity of arms, and on the 22nd and 23rd of February a body of men, supposed to number from 1,500 to 2,500, under Van Rensselaer, took possession of Hickory Island, in the St. Lawrence, about sixteen miles below Kingston and only two miles from Gananoque, where there was a small garrison of regulars and militia. A smaller party crossed from Buffalo to Point Abino at the same time. There was no movement, however, to co-operate with them anywhere in Canada. On the contrary, the militia assembled with great alacrity to repel them and in the course of a very few days the invaders retired. After his repulse at Fighting Island, McLeod removed his headquarters to Sandusky, Ohio, whence he despatched four hundred men under Colonels Seward and Bradley across the ice in sleighs to take possession of Pelee Island. After being there a few days they were attacked by Colonel John Maitland with five companies of the 32nd Regiment and nearly 200 Essex Militia and some volunteer cavalry under Lieut.-Colonel John Prince. Advancing in person at the head of the main body against their position at the north end of the island, Maitland detached Captain Brown with two companies of the 32nd by a circuitous route to the south end to cut off their retreat. Retiring before Maitland's force in their sleighs much more rapidly than it could follow, the invaders came suddenly upon Brown's detachment, which they greatly outnumbered, and taking shelter behind the piles of ice along the shore, they opened a most effective fire. Brown gallantly charged their position with the bayonet, dislodging them with the loss of Captains Van Rensselaer and McKeon and eleven men killed and nine prisoners. The remainder ran to their sleighs and escaped across the ice, carrying with them a considerable number of wounded men. Brown had lost two men killed and twenty-eight wounded in this very gallant affair. The same evening Colonel Prince captured General

Sutherland and his aid-de-camp, Captain Spencer, on their way to the island.

Early in June an attempt was made to raise the standard of rebellion in the Township of Pelham, in the County of Lincoln. Benjamin Wait, a native of the United States but a naturalized British subject, who had fled from Canada to escape arrest, was the chief organizer of this enterprise. A body of 526 men, well armed and equipped, was assembled in Buffalo, and small parties were sent secretly across the river with instructions to assemble at Aaron Winchester's farm, in the region known as the Short Hills. They took possession of a commanding position, which they rudely fortified, and spent eight days there beating for recruits and collecting provisions before their presence became known to the officers in command on that frontier. Their movements were generally made by night with the utmost secrecy and caution. Winchester and some of his immediate neighbors were active sympathizers, and the exact locality of the camp could not be easily ascertained. Their attempts to subvert the loyalty of the mass of the inhabitants proved quite unsuccessful, and they were joined only by a few settlers and some dissolute fellows who were probably attracted by the hope of plunder. After they had been there a few days, Colonel James Morrow, or Moreau, a tanner by trade, who was said to have had some military training, arrived and took command. A detachment of lancers advanced about the same time from Niagara to observe their movements, and pushed forward an outpost to occupy the little village of St. John's, about three miles from their position in the Short Hills. Having ascertained the strength of this party, and that it was quite unsupported, Morrow advanced with his whole force on the night of June 18th. Fourteen lancers, under Cornet Heath, were quartered in Overholt's tavern, a small wooden building, where they defended themselves obstinately until it was riddled with bullets, and preparations were made to set it on fire, when they surrendered.

The rapid advance of the remainder of the lancers and a troop of militia cavalry from St. Catharines next day, forced them to release their prisoners, abandon their camp and disperse. Many succeeded in escaping to the United States. A few were killed in the pursuit, and Morrow, Wait and thirty-seven others were apprehended. Twenty were found guilty and sentenced to death, but only the unfortunate Morrow was executed.

Between the 1st and 10th of November, about twenty of the Hunter's Lodges, in the State of New York, nearest the St. Lawrence River, began concentrating their forces for an attack upon Prescott, where fortifications were in course of construction. On the morning of the 11th, two schooners, in tow of the steamer United States, having about 600 men on board, with a quantity of military stores, left Millen's Bay below Sackett's Harbor. They touched at Ogdensburg, where General Bierge, who commanded, opportunely fell ill and went ashore. When they again started, one of the schooners, commanded by the notorious Bill Johnson, grounded on a shoal, and the steamer United States was prevented from entering the river by the British steamer Experiment, commanded by Lieut. Forvell, R. N., which lay in wait for her below. The other schooner alone, conveying 170 men, under Colonel Van Schultz, a Polish refugee, crossed the river and landed this party at the windmill below the town of Prescott. The windmill itself was a circular stone building, eighty feet in height, with walls over three feet in thickness. Near it were several other stone buildings surrounded by a low stone wall, forming an extremely defensible position against any force unprovided with artillery. The steamer Paul Pry afterwards attempted to tow across the schooner that had run aground, but as soon as she fairly got within Canadian waters the Experiment opened fire upon her with grape and canister. The Paul Pry left the schooner to her fate, and put back to Ogdensburg. Lieut. Forvell then ran his vessel down upon the schooner with the intention of taking possession of her, when he found himself in shoal water, and saw the steamer United States bearing down upon him. A brisk interchange of shots followed, during which the schooner escaped into Ogdensburg, and the United States soon followed, having received a cannon ball through one of her engines and several others in her hull. That night Captain Sandom, R. N., arrived from Kingston with the steamers Queen Victoria and Cobourg, having on board seventy marines and regulars. A detachment of the Glengarry militia, under Captain George Macdonell, came from below, and lay on the ground amid a heavy rain all night. Lieut.-Colonel O. R. Gowan, with 140 men of the 9th Provincial Battalion, also marched into Prescott during the night. Next morning the 2nd Battalion of Dundas militia, commanded by Lieut.Colonel John Crysler, nearly 300 strong, and detachments of the 1st and 2nd Grenville Battalions, under Lieut.-Colonel R. D. Fraser, also arrived. Colonel Plomer Young, Inspecting Field Officer, assumed the command, and determined upon an immediate attack. The left wing, composed of thirty marines under Lieut. Parker, Captain Macdonell's Glengarry militia, and some of the Grenville and Dundas militia, commanded by Lieut.-Colonel Fraser, drove the enemy's picquets out of the woods on that flank in gallant style. The right column, commanded by Colonel Young in person, consisting of forty men of 83rd Regiment, Lieut.-Colonel Gowan's battalion, and the remainder of the Dundas militia, advanced along the bank of the river, driving the enemy from behind the walls of the enclosures until they took shelter in the mill and adjacent buildings, but being much exposed during their operations their loss was severe. As they approached the mill the fire from its upper windows became very steady and accurate, and his men fell so fast under it that Colonel Young resolved to discontinue active operations until artillery could be obtained.

The mill was closely blockaded on the land side by Colonel Young, while the Experiment continued to patrol the river. Von Schultz sent a man across the river on a plank during the night to ask that boats should be sent to take off his men. Twenty-four hours later the Paul Pry actually crossed the river for that purpose, but a council of war decided to maintain the position, and instead of bringing away the invaders a small reinforcement was landed. At noon on the 16th, Colonel Henry Dundas, R. A., arrived from Kingston with a detachment of Royal Artillery in charge of three heavy guns, and five companies of the 83rd Regiment. The guns were planted on a rise of ground about 400 yards from the mill and their fire soon became effective. At the same time Captain Sandom, with two gunboats and a steamer began a bombardment of the enemy's position from the river. As it grew dark the troops gradually advanced, and Von Schultz, who had undertaken to defend one of the stone buildings outside the mill with only ten men, because none of his subordinates would venture to do it, was driven from his position and obliged to seek shelter among the bushes at the water's edge, where he was taken prisoner with some others. Every building near the mill that would burn was then set on fire, and as the flames blazed up fiercely about them the trembling garrison hung out a white flag. By this time all the troops were terribly exasperated and Colonel Dundas appears to have had great difficulty in restraining their fire. "To his determined resolution indeed," wrote Sir George Arthur, the Lieutenant-Governor, "it is to be ascribed that the militia of the country gave any quarter to the brigands; nothing, I believe, but the presence of the regular troops having saved any of them from being cut to pieces. The prisoners numbered one hundred and fifty seven, and upwards of forty of the invaders were supposed to have been killed. Their flag, on which was embroidered an eagle and a single star with the inscription "Liberated by the Onondaga Hunters," was captured. The British loss in these operations was two officers and eleven rank and file killed and four officers and sixty-three non commissioned officers and men wounded. Lieut. Delmage, of the 2nd Grenville Militia, four of the Loyal Glengarry Highlanders and four of the 2nd Dundas Militia were among the killed, and Lieut.-Colonel Gowan of the Ninth Provincial Battalion, Ensign Angus Macdonnell of the Loyal Glengarry Highlanders, Lieutenant John Parlow and seven men of the 2nd Dundas Militia were wounded.

One object of the descent upon Prescott was undoubtedly to create a diversion in favor of insurrection at Beauharnois and simultaneous invasion from the United States at Odelstown and Rouse's Point. To restore order and repel the the invaders Sir John Colborne had again summoned the militia of the Eastern districts of Upper Canada to his assistance. Between the 5th and 9th of November three regiments of Glengary militia, under Colonels Donald Macdonnell, Alexander Chisholm and Alexander Fraser, and a regiment of Stormount militia under Colonel Donald Æneas Macdonell, assembled and marched to Coteau du Lac. On the 10th of November these regiments, numbering more than 1000 men, crossed the St. Lawrence to Hungry Bay, and marched upon Beauharnois in conjunction with 150 regulars. The insurgents were dispersed with trifling loss, and a steamer they had seized was retaken.

Four days later, when the landing of the enemy at Prescott became known, they were ordered to return to Upper Canada, but they arrived too late to take any part in the attack on the windmill; they were, however, stationed as a garrison at Prescott and Cornwall during the winter.

"Hunters" in considerable numbers had assembled at or near Detroit, not only from other parts of Michigan, but from the principal cities in the States of Ohio and New York. The steamer Champlain was engaged and stores collected for an expedition. On the night of December 3rd four hundred men marched openly through the streets of Detroit, within sight of the sentinels at the armory, and embarked without hindrance. At 3 a. m., next morning, they landed at Pelette's farm, four miles above Windsor, which was then occupied by one company of Essex militia, commanded by Captain Lewis. The invaders advanced rapidly, and were not discovered until they were within a quarter of a mile of the barracks, which they immediately surrounded. The militia fired briskly upon their assailants, but were soon driven back into their barracks, which

Sir Allan McNab.

were then set on fire. Ten or twelve rushed out and made their escape, thirteen were taken prisoners, and two wounded men were supposed to have perished in the burning buildings.

The enemy had advanced to the centre of the town in two columns, under Colonels Putnam and Howell, and occupied a position in Francis Baby's orchard. Bierce remained with the reserve some distance in the rear. After firing a single volley, Captain Sparke charged the invaders, who were believed to number about 130, and drove them headlong through the town. Both Putnam and Howell were killed, and their flag was captured by Ensign Rankin, of the Incorporated Militia. Sparke lost only one man killed and one wounded in this gallant attack. Colonel Prince, being then informed that a body of the

33

enemy were advancing upon Sandwich, recalled his men from the pursuit and marched back to that place, affording General Bierce a welcome opportunity to escape to the American side of the river with most of his men. Twenty-one of the invaders had been killed. Four, who were brought in as prisoners at the close of the action, were shot as outlaws by Prince's orders. Forty-six others were afterwards taken, and numbers were supposed to have perished in the woods. The whole loss of the militia was four killed and four wounded.

Between the 5th of December, 1837, and the 1st of November, 1838, including the prisoners taken on the schooner Ann, at Point au Pelee, and the Short Hills, 885 persons had been arrested on a charge of treason or insurrection; of these, three, Peter Matthews, Samuel Lount and James Morrow, had been executed, sixty-five had been sentenced to terms of imprisonment, or to be transported or banished from the Province, forty-seven had been tried and acquitted, twenty-seven (chiefly persons taken in arms at Pelee Island or the Short Hills) were yet in custody, and 743 had been dismissed without trial or pardoned. Sixty-one persons who had left the Province were indicted.

The militia called into service at this period has been estimated at not less than 40,000. Besides 106 regiments of country militia there were five battalions of Incorporated Militia, which were not finally disbanded until 1843, twelve Provincial Battalions on duty for a stated period, and thirty-one corps of artillery, cavalry, and rifles.

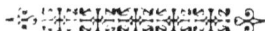

Chapter IV

TWENTY YEARS of unbroken peace elapsed, during which the necessity for any armed force in addition to the regular troops in garrison was scarcely obvious. The war with Russia caused a revival of military ardor, and in 1855 an "Act to regulate the Militia" was passed by which the enrollment of volunteers as active militia was authorized, and the provinces were divided into military districts for that purpose. "The active militia," this act read, "shall consist of volunteer troops of cavalry, field batteries and foot companies of artillery and companies of infantry armed as riflemen, but not exceeding in the whole sixteen troops of cavalry, seven field batteries of artillery, five foot companies of artillery and fifty companies of riflemen, not to exceed five thousand men." The Act came into force on July 1st, 1855, and was to continue in operation "for three years, and from thence until the end of the next ensuing session of Parliament of the Province and no longer, provided that if, at the time when this act would otherwise expire, there should happen to be war between Her Majesty and the United States of America, then this Act shall continue in force until the end of the session of the Provincial Parliament next after the proclamation of peace between Her Majesty and the said United States."

Until then, the annual muster and inspection of the County Militia, comprising practically the whole male population of the country, between the ages of 18 and 45, continued to be held, to the great inconvenience of all concerned, particularly in the rural districts where many persons had to travel great distances to attend, and lose several days' time. It had become a wretched burlesque. Neither officers or men, with perhaps a few exceptions, were armed, equipped, or in any way instructed in the military duties they were presumed to perform. The organization consisted solely of a list of officers. The new act was so far successful that the full number of corps authorized were organized and equipped (largely at their own expense), and in many cases appear to have attained a creditable degree of proficiency in troop or company drill, under instructions from the regular service.

Hamilton was one of the first cities to take advantage of the act. Two rifle companies and a field battery were organized before the end of the year, and in 1856 a Highland company of infantry was added, chiefly by the exertions of Captain (afterwards Lieut.-Colonel) James Aitchison Skinner, who uniformed it at his own expense.

Another militia act, which became law in 1859, provided for the organization of battalions of infantry and rifles wherever practicable. The prospect of hostilities with the United States, in consequence of the outrage on the steamer Trent, occasioned great excitement, and gave a decided stimulus to the volunteer movement all over Canada. The Governor-General appointed a Royal Commission to report on the most effective means of organizing the militia for the defence of the country. The Commissioners strongly recommended that a force of 50,000 men should be embodied and trained for twenty-eight days every year.

The excitement had not altogether subsided when the general order of December 13th, 1862, was published, authorizing the formation of a battalion of infantry in Hamilton, designated as the Thirteenth. The two existing rifle companies, then commanded by Captains James Edwin O'Reilly and Stephen T. Cattley, were incorporated in the battalion as numbers one and two, and the Highland company, under Captain Skinner, as number three company. Four new companies were formed under command of Captains John Brown, George Herve Mingaye, Donald McInnes and Thomas Bell. Hon. Isaac Buchanan, the most eminent public man in the city, was gazetted as Lieutenant-Colonel Commanding. Captains Skinner and O'Reilly were promoted to be Majors almost immediately. The ranks were soon filled with enthusiastic volunteers, and on the 19th of December, 1862, an eighth company was added under Captain John McKeown, and on the 9th of January, 1863, a ninth, commanded by Captain Robert Law. The former company was, however, disbanded on the 10th of July, 1863.

A fund of $4,000 was rapidly raised by public subscription, and in March, 1863, the construction of a commodious drill shed was begun, which was completed in time for a battalion parade on the 4th of June. It was designed by, and constructed under the supervision of an officer of the battalion, Lieutenant afterwards Major) Alexander H. Askin.

The use of the motto "Semper Paratus" was authorized, and on the 1st

36

of September, 1863, the Battalion was presented with colors by Mrs. Buchanan, wife of the commanding officer. The escort on that occasion was commanded by Captain John Stewart Henderson, Ensigns Watson and Buchanan being detailed to carry the colors. These were duly consecrated by Reverend J. Gamble Geddes, the Rector of Christ's Church, and received from Mrs. Buchanan by Major Skinner.

On September 3rd the battalion, commanded by Major Skinner, numbering about three hundred officers and men, took part in a review at Brantford,

THIRTEENTH BATTALION OF INFANTRY ON PARADE GROUND, MAY 24TH, 1899.

where nearly 2,300 volunteers of the district were inspected by Major General George Napier. The Thirteenth was the strongest battalion on parade, and was equally distinguished for general proficiency in drill. The officers present were Major Skinner, Captains Henderson, Cattley, Mingaye, Bell and Law, Lieuts. Papps, Macrae, Askin, Hilton, Biggar and Wink, Ensigns Watson, Buchanan, Irving, Jamieson and Inkson.

On the 13th of January, 1864, Lieut.-Colonel Hoste, C. B., R. A., was appointed Inspector of Militia for the district, and made the first official inspection

37

of the Battalion a few weeks later. On December 30th of that year Lieut.-Colonel Buchanan retired from the command, and on January 27th, 1865, was succeeded by Lieut.-Colonel Alfred Booker, who had commanded the Hamilton Field Battery since its organization in 1855, and enjoyed the reputation of an energetic and efficient officer. In April of this year, three Administrative Battalions for frontier service were organized mainly to prevent a recurrence of inroads upon the territory of the United States, by refugees from the South, similar to the famous St. Alban's Raid. Lieut.-Colonel Booker was then selected for the command of the second of these battalions, having its headquarters at Niagara, and he appointed Captain (afterwards Lieut.-Colonel) Henry Erskine Irving, of his own battalion, to be Adjutant, Captain John Henery succeeding him. A company composed of volunteers from the Thirteenth was enlisted, and officered by Captain Cattley, Lieut. Watson and Ensign Jamieson. It was sent to Prescott, where it formed part of the Eastern Administrative Battalion, and remained in garrison until November, when its term of service expired. Another company was immediately formed to take its place by Captain Irving, having Ensigns Grant and Hebden as his subalterns, and proceeded to Windsor. Ensign Grant was appointed Adjutant of the Western Administrative Battalion during his term of service.

On the 10th of November, 1865, No. 7 company, and, on the 15th of December, No. 8 company, were disbanded, and the establishment of the battalion reduced to six companies of fifty-five non-commissioned officers and men, No. 9 becoming No. 3.

During the autumn of 1865, and the following winter, rumors prevailed of formidable preparations for an invasion of Canada from the United States by bodies of men professing to act under the instructions of the Executive of the Fenian or Irish Republican Brotherhood, who were known to have collected large sums of money for some such purpose. As nearly a million of soldiers lately engaged in the civil war had just disbanded, many of whom were naturally disinclined to return to a life of peaceful toil, a formidable army of well trained men, it was confidently expected, could be easily assembled for any enterprise that promised adventure or profit. To many enthusiasts the conquest of Canada doubtless seemed an easy undertaking at the time. The reports of consuls and other confidential agents in the principal American cities satisfied the Canadian Government that there was genuine cause for alarm, and on the 7th of March, 1866, the Executive Council determined to call out 10,000 volunteers, which was done that day by telegraph. The entire Thirteenth Battalion was included in this force, but permitted to remain at its headquarters, performing daily drills and mounting guards at the drill shed, artillery gun sheds, magazine, and the Mountain View Hotel, in constant expectation of being moved to the frontier.

Everywhere throughout the province the most admirable spirit was displayed by the mass of the people. Commenting on this subject only two days after the call for volunteers was issued, the Governor-General, Lord Monck, wrote to the Colonial Secretary :

" I may also mention that offers of service continue to be received at head-quarters to an extent far beyond the number of men required, and I have no doubt, should the occasion unfortunately arise, the supply of volunteers who would present themselves for the defense of the country would be limited only by the numbers of the male population capable of bearing arms."

It was generally expected that the 17th of March would be distinguished by the first hostile movement, and as that day passed without any attempt at invasion, the alarm gradually abated. A few days later a General Order was published, relieving the volunteers on service at their regimental headquarters from daily parade, but requiring them to perform two days' drill in the week, and to continue in readiness to move at a moment's notice.

On the 8th of May, 1866, the Battalion was inspected by Major-General Napier, who was so well pleased with its appearance that he caused Lieut.-Colonel Durie, the Assistant Adjutant-General, to write the following letter to Lieut.-Colonel Booker :

TORONTO, 8th May, 1866.

SIR, I am directed by Major General Napier, C. B., commanding 1st Military District, C. W., to express to you the gratification he felt at the very creditable and solderlike appearance made by the Volunteer Militia Force under your command, when inspected by the Major-General this day. Their steadiness under arms, and the manner in which they moved on parade, merits this expression of the Major-General's approbation, which you will be good enough to convey to the force under your command."

CHAPTER V

A SMALL volunteer force which had been stationed at Port Colborne since the 10th of March to protect the Welland Canal, was relieved from duty on the 21st of April, 1866, and sent home. The regular troops in Western Ontario, consisting of the 16th and 47th Regiments, and a battery of Royal Artillery, were stationed at Toronto, Hamilton and London. The Fenian organization was still known to be active in all the large cities of the Northern States, but so many rumors of invasion had resulted in nothing that few persons believed that they would ever attempt to cross the frontier. In Buffalo they were particularly numerous, and several companies of "Irish Rifles" had drilled publicly during the winter. Many lines of railway entered that city from the east, south and west, and a large body of unarmed men could easily be concentrated there without attracting much attention, and boats for transporting them to Canada could be hired without exciting the suspicions of the officers of the Federal Government, who were not generally supposed to be particularly anxious to thwart their plans. When the volunteers were withdrawn from Port Colborne, there was no body of troops under arms nearer than Hamilton. No opposition need therefore be anticipated in crossing the river, and a single day's march might put the invaders in possession of the Welland Canal.

During the last week in May considerable bodies of men, who seemed to be acting in concert, were observed moving towards the Canadian frontier along the principal lines of railway in the United States. They were unarmed and dressed in plain clothes, and, when questioned as to their destination, uniformly replied that they were on their way to the gold mines of California.

One body of 115 men, commanded by Colonel John O'Neill, left Nashville, Tennessee, on May 27th. At Louisville, Kentucky, he was joined by Colonel

40

Owen Starr with 144 men, and at Indianapolis by Captain Haggerty with a hundred men. On the night of the 28th they arrived at Cleveland, where they expected to cross the lake, but were ordered by telegram to proceed to Buffalo, which they reached on the morning of the 30th. The men were at once billeted in small squads in various parts of the city to evade suspicion. A very large and enthusiastic Fenian mass meeting had been held in St. James' Hall the night before, at which the invasion of Canada had been publicly discussed. It is stated on good authority that maps of the British Provinces were exhibited, and the ardor of the audience was stimulated by a general invitation to select

OFFICERS OF THE THIRTEENTH BATTALION OF INFANTRY MAY, 1899.

the farms they wanted after the conquest was effected. The excitement of the local Fenians was accordingly at fever-heat.

On the night of the 31st it is believed that at least 1,500 men assembled at their drill-halls and other places of rendezvous, many of them already armed and equipped. Before midnight they again separated into small parties, but instead of returning to their homes and lodgings as usual, they marched rapidly, by different routes, to the suburb of Lower Black Rock, about five miles from the heart of the city, where several canal boats and a steam tug lay in readiness to convey them across the river, and nine waggons loaded with arms and accoutrements were also waiting their arrival. Brigadier General Lynch had been appointed to the command of the expedition, but as he did not arrive, Colonel O'Neill took his place. O'Neill was a gallant and efficient soldier, who had served for eight years, first in the regular and then in the volunteer army of the United States. He had fought his way from the ranks to the rank of Captain, and had been recommended for further promotion when the civil war came to an end. He was a sincere and unselfish enthusiast. His justification of the enterprise is brief and candid : " You recognize the English government as your government, and the English flag as your flag. We desired to destroy both. You were ready to defend both ; hence our only cause of quarrel with you. If we had been able we would not have hesitated to kill every soldier who was ready to fight for England."

The number of men reported to him in readiness to cross the river at that time was only eight hundred. Many of these men were veterans of the civil war, some of whom still wore the blue or grey uniform of their respective armies. The resident Fenians of the city failed to appear in any considerable numbers. The passage of the river was easily accomplished, and at four o'clock on the morning of June 1st, four canal boats filled with men were safely moored at the Lower Ferry Dock, two miles below the village of Fort Erie. The number that actually crossed at this time, according to O'Neill's account, did not exceed six hundred. Lord Monck's letter to Mr. Cardwell, based probably upon information telegraphed from Buffalo, agrees with this estimate exactly. Their landing was first noticed by some country people who had been spearing fish by torchlight, and they spread the alarm as they hurried home. O'Neill ordered the telegraph wires to be cut, and sent Colonel Starr with a detachment to occupy Fort Erie village and take possession of the railway yard near the old fort. This was effected about sunrise but not before the officials of the Buffalo and Lake Huron Railway had succeeded in removing all their rolling stock in one huge train. A small party on a hand car pursued them for six miles up the line, and burnt the bridge at Sauerwein's over the Six Mile Creek. O'Neill made a requisition for provisions upon the Reeve of the village, but assured him that no depredations would be committed by his men. His demand was complied with, and at 10 o'clock he marched his whole force down the river to the mouth of Frenchman's Creek, about a mile below his landing place, where he encamped and awaited reinforcements. But the United States steamer Michigan had entered the river, and prevented the remainder of the force that had assembled at Black Rock from crossing in a body. Small unarmed parties passed over on the ferry that still continued to ply between Upper Black Rock and Fort Erie village, and a few are said to have crossed in small boats. These accessions may have increased his strength for the moment to 800 or 900, as estimated by the British Consul. Still, another telegram from Buffalo

42

FIELD AND STAFF OFFICERS OF THE THIRTEENTH BATTALION OF INFANTRY.

1. LIEUT.-COLONEL H. McLAREN, COMMANDING
2. MAJOR J. STONEMAN.   3. MAJOR E. G. ZEALAND   4. HON. MAJOR J. J. MASON, PAYMASTER.
5. SURGEON-MAJOR H. S. GRIFFIN, M. D.   6. CAPTAIN AND ADJUTANT W. O. TIDSWELL.
7. SURGEON-CAPTAIN G. S. RENNIE, M. D.
8. CAPTAIN T. W. LESTER, QUARTERMASTER.   9. REV. G. A. FORNERET, M. A., CHAPLAIN.

asserted that 1,340 men had then crossed with six field guns and 2,500 stand of arms, and that by next morning they fully expected to be joined by all the men they could arm. This false statement unquestionably had its effect next day on the movements of the British troops.

Foraging parties were sent out in all directions to obtain provisions and to seize horses and cattle. They found most of the neighboring farmhouses deserted by their inhabitants, who had generally removed their horses, but they secured a sufficient number to mount their field officers and a party of scouts. During the afternoon Captain Donohue, commanding one of these parties, who had advanced several miles along the river road, reported that he had seen British scouts who at once retired. Later on Colonel Hoy was sent out on the same road and encountered, as he thought, a party of scouts six miles from camp. O'Neill had been joined by Major John C. Canty, a Fenian, who had taken up his residence in Fort Erie about a year before, and seems to have been his principal agent in obtaining intelligence. How this was managed can only be conjectured. At all events the Fenian leader knew, at 8 p. m., that two columns of troops were advancing against him, the stronger by way of Chippawa, composed of regular troops and volunteers, the other by way of Port Colborne, consisting of volunteers only.

At ten o'clock that night he seems to have abandoned all hope of receiving further reinforcements. He destroyed his spare arms and began his march down the river road towards Chippawa. After advancing in this direction about four miles he turned westward on the road separating the townships of Bertie and Willoughby, and moved along it until he crossed the Erie and Niagara Railway, when he allowed his men to lie down in the fields between the railway and the right bank of Black Creek. This was a very secluded spot, as there were no houses within a mile, and the road was little travelled. It is possible that he may have expected that the column of troops at Chippawa would attempt to advance by rail during the night and intended to waylay them as they crossed Black Creek. It must then have been nearly midnight. He states that his force had been already reduced by desertion to about five hundred. Some of the deserters had recrossed the river and others remained about Fort Erie. This statement is partly substantiated by the large number of stragglers captured at that place next day. Within a few hours he seems to have received further information, for at three o'clock he roused his men and after allowing them to breakfast he marched rapidly southward until he struck the Ridge Road, which winds southwesterly from the river to Lake Erie, along the summit of a bold ridge of limestone rock which crops out of the ground in many places. His object, he explains, was "to get between the two columns, and if possible defeat one of them before the other could come to its assistance." The column advancing from Port Colborne was the weaker in every respect and

44

COCHRAN, PHOTO.

CAPTAINS OF THE THIRTEENTH BATTALION OF INFANTRY.

1. CAPTAIN AND BREVET MAJOR E. E. W. MOORE.
2. CAPTAIN AND BREVET MAJOR S. C. MEWBURN.   3. CAPTAIN AND BREVET MAJOR F. B. ROSS.
4. CAPTAIN R. H. LABATT.   5. CAPTAIN J. H. HERRING.   6. CAPTAIN C. A. P. POWIS.
7. CAPTAIN G. D. FEARMAN.   8 CAPTAIN W. H. BRUCE.

he had decided to strike it where he expected that its advance would be checked by the destruction of the railway bridge below Ridgeway.

On the evening of the 31st of May, instructions had been received in Hamilton and Toronto to assemble the volunteer force of those cities at an early hour next morning in readiness to proceed to the frontier. Before daylight orders came directing their movements. From Toronto eight companies of the Queen's Own Rifles embarked in a steamer for Port Dalhousie, with instructions to proceed at once by rail to Port Colborne. The two remaining companies followed later in the day by the same route. At noon three companies of the 47th Regiment and a battery of Royal Artillery went by rail through Hamilton to Niagara Falls, followed at 4 p. m. by a second train conveying two more companies of the 47th and the Tenth Battalion of Active Militia.

The Thirteenth assembled at 7 o'clock a. m., but did not entrain until nearly ten, when they were sent to Dunnville by way of Paris, arriving about 3 p. m. They detrained and were billeted in the village. They were joined by the York and Caledonia rifle companies from the County of Haldimand, under Captains Robert H. Davis and Jackson. In the evening the whole force was moved forward by rail to Port Colborne, arriving at 11 p. m. From Hamilton, also, 200 men of the 16th Regiment were sent forward by rail to Niagara Falls. When these movements were completed, a force of about 900 volunteers was assembled at Port Colborne, composed of the Queen's Own Rifles, 480 men, Thirteenth Battalion, 265 men, York and Caledonia Rifles, 95 men, Welland Canal Field Battery (acting as infantry), 60 men, and a regular force at Niagara Falls, consisting of 200 men of the 16th Regiment, 200 of the 47th, and a battery of Royal Artillery, under Colonel Peacocke, of the 16th. As the enemy was reported moving upon Chippawa, Peacocke pushed forward that evening to secure the bridge, his infantry proceeding by rail, and the artillery following by road, as no cars could be procured to convey it. Chippawa was occupied about 9 p. m., and at 4.30 a. m. Peacocke was joined by 150 men of the 47th, the Tenth Battalion, 415 men, and the Nineteenth Battalion, 350 men. The distance between Chippawa and Port Colborne by the shortest route is about fifteen miles, and shortly before midnight Colonel Peacocke despatched Captain Akers, R. E., across the country with instructions to the commandant at that place to form a junction with his column at Stevensville next day at 10 a. m., but does not seem to have indicated the route he wished him to pursue.

The long train of rolling stock that had escaped from Fort Erie jumped the track and was wrecked three miles east of Port Colborne, but during the day the road was cleared, and a party sent down under escort to repair Sauerwein's bridge. Mr. Larmour, the Superintendent, went on in a hand-car to Fort Erie, where he arrived at 10 p. m., and found the place not only unoccu-

LIEUTENANTS OF THE THIRTEENTH BATTALION.

1. LIEUTENANT J. D. LAIDLAW.   2. LIEUTENANT F. R. WADDELL.   3. LIEUTENANT W. A. LOGIE.
4. LIEUTENANT C. G. BARKER.   5. LIEUTENANT W. R. MARSHALL.
6. LIEUTENANT R. A. ROBERTSON.   7. LIEUTENANT A. K. McLAREN.   8. LIEUTENANT W. L. ROSS.

pied by the Fenians, but practically deserted. He met Mr. Richard Graham, Collector of Customs, who had visited the Fenian camp and seen, as he supposed, their whole force. There was no indication of any movement on their part when he came away, and he had seen a good many drunken men. Mr. Larmour persuaded Mr. Graham to accompany him to Port Colborne. On returning to Sauerwein's he found that the bridge had been made passable for trains, and the line was accordingly again opened to Fort Erie. With this information he returned to Port Colborne before midnight. When Colonel Booker arrived there with the troops from Dunnville, he found Lieut.-Colonel J. S. Dennis, Brigade Major of the District, in command, whom he outranked and superseded. The wildest rumors were in circulation, and the Queen's Own and Field Battery were standing under arms in the streets. After listening to Mr. Graham's statement, Colonels Booker and Dennis decided upon a plan of operations by which they hoped to cut off the retreat of the Fenians and ensure the capture or destruction of their whole force. Eighty men, composed of the Welland Field Battery and Dunnville Naval Brigade, were to embark in the steam-tug Robb, proceed down the lake to Fort Erie and patrol the river, while the remainder of his column would advance at once by rail as far as practicable and unite with Colonel Peacocke next day in a general attack on the enemy's camp. While they were yet consulting, Captain Akers arrived and was induced to consent to their plan. At 3 a. m., a telegram, announcing their decision, was despatched to Colonel Peacocke, and without waiting for a reply the men were embarked on the Robb. Colonel Dennis, and Captain Akers himself, went on board, and the tug steamed out of the harbor. The troops were entrained and on the point of moving, when at 3.45 a. m., a peremptory message was received from Colonel Peacocke saying that his original instructions must be adhered to, and a junction formed at Stevensville. Colonel Booker was directed to leave Port Colborne at 7 a. m. It was deemed useless to detrain as the troops had no quarters to go to. Some of the men were noisy, and there was little sleep for anybody. At 5 a. m. the order was given for the train to pull out. The force under Lieut.-Colonel Booker, nominally 840 of all ranks, probably did not exceed 800 effectives. They had been under arms for twenty-four hours in a state of intense excitement, fatigued by travel, deprived of sleep and insufficiently fed. They were without blankets, knapsacks, haversacks, mess tins or water bottles, and the only means they possessed of carrying their overcoats was by wearing them. The only horse with the column was ridden by Lieut.-Colonel Booker, and had to be taken to Ridgeway in a mail car. No attempt seems to have been made to mount the other officers. There were no means provided for transporting the reserve ammunition after leaving the train. There was no ambulance party, nor hospital corps, except three surgeons, one of whom was not in uniform, and carried his instruments in a hand-bag.

48

SECOND LIEUTENANTS OF THE THIRTEENTH BATTALION.

1. LIEUTENANT A. F. ZIMMERMAN.   2. LIEUTENANT J. AMBREY.   3. LIEUTENANT A. E. MASON.
4. LIEUTENANT P. DOMVILLE.   5. LIEUTENANT G. J. HENDERSON.
6. LIEUTENANT J. A. TURNER.   7. LIEUTENANT E. V. WRIGHT.   8. LIEUTENANT A. PAIN.

Shortly before six o'clock the train arrived at Ridgeway, where it was determined to detrain as the nearest point to Stevensville. This village consisted of a single hotel, a couple of stores, and about twenty houses. It was almost deserted, and few of the soldiers were able to procure anything to stay their hunger. Some time was necessarily consumed in forming and inspecting the troops and distributing ammunition. Although the necessary waggons undoubtedly could have been obtained by a proper effort to convey it with the column, all the reserve ammunition was ordered back to Port Colborne on the train. While preparations for the march were still in progress, some horsemen rode in with information that the Fenians were not far distant on the Ridge Road, but their warning was unheeded. This story indeed seemed improbable, as they were known to be encamped at the mouth of Frenchman's Creek, ten miles away, at nine o'clock the night before. Yet these men had actually seen an advance party of Fenians, and had been mistaken by them for mounted scouts. This was reported to O'Neill, and at the same time the sound of bugles and the whistles of a locomotive was heard in the direction of Ridgeway. He continued to advance until he definitely ascertained that troops were approaching along the Ridge Road, when he occupied a position on the Bertie road, running eastward to Fort Erie. His right flank rested on a brick house, with wooden barn and other outbuildings, surrounded by a garden and small orchard, at the intersection of this road with the Ridge Road, and his line extended eastward five or six hundred yards, curving forward into a strip of woods to flank the advance of his assailants as they approached along the Ridge Road, or over the open ground to the right. The fence in front was strengthened with additional rails and other available materials. A small reserve was stationed in an orchard some three hundred yards in the rear, and a weak line of skirmishers was thrown forward, nearly half a mile, under Colonel Owen Starr. O'Neill's force probably numbered between five and eight hundred men, but they were the pick of his command, inured to fatigue and hardship, and accustomed to fighting under cover. They probably had not had much to eat since their landing, but to many of them that was no new experience. They were desperate men, thoroughly alert, and ready for action.

Colonel Booker advanced along the Ridge Road in a column of fours, the Queen's Own, under Major Gilmore, leading, followed by the Thirteenth, commanded by Major Skinner, and the York and Caledonia rifle companies. The sun was hot and the road dusty. After marching a little more than a mile armed men were seen lurking behind trees and fences. A company of the Queen's Own, armed with Spencer repeating rifles, was ordered to extend. Some shots were fired, and two other companies of the same battalion were sent forward, on the double, to prolong the firing line on either flank. Within ten minutes the fire became rapid and continuous. The Fenian skirmishers were steadily forced back, or retired intentionally, reserving their fire until their pursuers attempted to cross a fence, or were checked by some other obstacle. After advancing in this manner for a few hundred yards it was discovered that the woods on the right were occupied by the enemy, and the University and Highland companies of the Queen's Own were extended to the right front to drive them out. Within fifteen or twenty minutes the firing line in front had got rid of all their ammunition to very little purpose beyond enveloping themselves in a dense cloud of smoke, under cover of which they had advanced, with trifling

loss, nearly half a mile. They were close upon O'Neill's temporary breastworks, where he had decided to make a determined stand. Here they were relieved by Numbers One, Two, and Three companies of the Thirteenth and the York rifle company, who moved forward very steadily to the assault of the enemy's position in extended order. Separated from them by an interval of two or three hundred yards, and forming an obtuse angle with the remainder of the firing line, were the University and Highland companies of the Queen's Own, still engaged with the enemy in the woods, whom they had failed to dispossess. On the Ridge Road, and in the fields on the right, about three hundred yards in rear of the firing line, formed as supports, were the remaining three companies of the Thirteenth and the Caledonia Rifles. About the same distance further to the rear were six com-

OFFICERS OF D COMPANY, 1866.

CAPT. JOHN BROWN.
ENSIGN JOHN B. YOUNG.   LIEUT. PERCY G. ROUTH.

panies of the Queen's Own in quarter column, three of whom had exhausted all their ammunition. After sending a message to Ridgeway to bring forward the reserve ammunition that he had sent away to Port Colborne, Colonel Booker seems to have dismounted and stationed himself near the reserve. From this position he could not possibly see what was going on in front, and he had not a single mounted officer with him to bring information or convey orders. His only means of transmitting commands to the force under his command was by sound of the bugle.

The new firing line advanced with so much vivacity that it is supposed the Fenians mistook them for regular troops. The York Rifles and some of the Thirteenth passed down into the fields below the shelf of rock along which the road winds, and, availing themselves of some slight cover of brushwood, turned the enemy's right flank. At all events the Fenians failed to make the resistance that might have been expected at this point. They gave ground and were briskly pursued. O'Neill states that he "fell back a few hundred yards and formed a new line." Some of his mounted officers came into view riding rapidly forward on the Ridge Road, and a party of horsemen was discovered about the same time at the turn of the road on the left, leading to Stevensville. The latter were inhabitants attracted by the sounds of battle. Some one hastily raised a cry of "cavalry," which was rapidly passed on to the rear. The firing line attempted to form rallying squares in the fields, and the supports and reserves did the same upon the road. The Fenians in front saw their advantage, and came on with loud yells, while their comrades in the woods directed their fire with considerable effect upon the square formed by the reserve. Scarcely had the squares been formed then the bugle, by Colonel Booker's orders, sounded "retire." In an instant all was confusion, and the retreat commenced in much haste and disorder. When No. 3 Company of the Thirteenth, which had been working around the enemy's right, after turning them out of their breastworks, regained the road, they saw their supports and reserves retreating in a confused mass. Majors Skinner and Cattley, and Captain Henery, were conspicuous in their efforts to hold the enemy in check. The two companies of the Queen's Own on the left were isolated for the moment, and lost seven men killed or wounded and two prisoners in coming off. The pursuit was not vigorously pushed, although the Fenians actually followed the retreating column as far as Ridgeway, whence it retired towards Port Colborne along the railway track. Colonel Booker seems to have at once abandoned all hopes of rallying his men and resuming the advance. When about half way to Port Colborne they met Mr. Larmour with an engine and two flat cars bringing up the reserve ammunition. By noon they were again at Port Colborne. The total loss on this occasion was too insignificant to account for the panic that occurred. One officer, one sergeant and seven men were killed, five officers and twenty-six rank and file wounded, several of whom fell into the hands of the enemy, with seven unwounded prisoners. In this, and the subsequent skirmish at Fort Erie, O'Neill stated his loss, as nearly as could be ascertained, at eight killed and fifteen wounded, but nine of his men were subsequently buried on the field by the inhabitants, and he left six severely wounded behind, besides removing several in waggons. Among the killed was Lieut. E. R. Lonergan, of Buffalo, and among the wounded left behind, Michael Cochrane, the color-sergeant of the Indianapolis Company, a very gallant fellow, who was conspicuous by leading the final charge.

After the action O'Neill lost no time in retreating. He did not even linger to bury his dead. Colonel Starr, with one column, marched down the railway to destroy the bridges, while O'Neill himself retired by the Garrison Road to Fort Erie. At that place he encountered the Welland Field Battery, and after a brief skirmish captured the greater part of it. During the night a tug and scow came over, in which the Fenians embarked, and escaped into American waters.

The loss of the Thirteenth Battalion was remarkably light, considering the heavy fire to which it was exposed for a considerable length of time. None were killed, and only one officer and six men wounded. These were Lieut. Percy Gore Routh (No. 4), and privates Edwin Hilder (No. 1), S. Dallas, J. G. Powell, James Stuart, Richard Pentecost (No. 3), George McKenzie (No. 4), and John Donnelly (No. 5). Privates James S. Greenhill and Joseph Simpson were taken prisoners; privates James Cahill, W. B. Nicolls (No. 1), Crossman, Henderson, Mason, Urquahart (No. 4), and Irvine (No. 6), were sent to the hospital after their arrival at Port Colborne, suffering from exhaustion or sunstroke. Privates Morrison, Laker and Cahill died of disease contracted in the campaign. The officers present in the action were Lieut.-Colonel Booker, Majors Skinner and Cattley; Captains Watson, Askin and Grant; Lieuts. Sewell, Ritchie, Routh, Ferguson and Gibson; Ensigns McKenzie, Baker, Armstrong, Roy and Young, and Captain and Adjutant Henery. The colors were borne by Ensigns Armstrong and Baker.

From the 2nd to 20th of June, 1866, the Thirteenth was quartered at Port Colborne, forming part of a small brigade of regulars and volunteers, commanded by Lieut.-Colonel Villiers, H. M. 47th Regiment. On August 10th, Lieut.-Colonel Booker, who had been effectually discredited by the unfortunate result of the action at Ridgeway, retired from the command and was succeeded by Major Skinner. Two months later the battalion proceeded to the camp at Thorold, where it was brigaded with the Queen's Own, the Twenty-Second Oxford Battalion, three companies of the 16th Regiment, and two batteries of Royal Artillery, under Colonel (now Field Marshal) Wolseley.

The Fenian Raid of 1866 once more demonstrated the unfaltering determination of the Canadian people to defend their frontier at all hazards. Lord Monck observed, in his dispatch of June 8th, they "responded instantaneously to the call to arms, and I am sure I do not exaggerate when I say that within twenty-four hours after the issue of the order, 20,000 men were under arms, and that within forty-eight hours after the same time they, in combination with the regular troops, were disposed by the Lieutenant-General commanding in positions which rendered the Province secure from attack."

Chapter VI

HE HISTORY of the Thirteenth, since the Fenian Raid of 1866, is mainly a record of conscientious, hard work at local headquarters and the rifle ranges, which has resulted in a long series of well-deserved triumphs with the rifle and at inspection.

In the summer of 1866, the muzzle-loading Enfield rifle, with which the Battalion had been armed since its organization, was replaced with the Spencer repeating rifle, but this was discarded in December, 1867, for the Snider Enfield breechloader.

By a general order of the 23rd of May, 1867, the Dundas Infantry Company, under Captain Wardell, and the Waterdown Infantry Company, under Captain Glasgow, were attached to the Thirteenth Battalion as Nos. 7 and 8. The annual drill for 1867 and 1868 was performed at local headquarters, and in the Adjutant General's report for the latter year the Thirteenth is specially distinguished as "a very good regiment, conduct good."

The ladies of Hamilton presented the Battalion, on March 4th, 1869, with a very valuable and appropriate drum-major's baton. The annual drill was that year once more performed at local headquarters, and the Adjutant General, Colonel Robertson Ross, in his official report, referred to the Thirteenth in the most gratifying terms.

"I afterwards inspected the Thirteenth Battalion, under the command of Lieutenant-Colonel Skinner, numbering 24 officers and 388 men. The inspection in the drill shed at Hamilton, in the evening, was attended by a large number of spectators. Lieutenant-Colonel Skinner is one of the most zealous officers in the active militia; he has devoted much time and money for the good of the service, and has succeeded in bringing his battalion to a very high state of efficiency.

"The appearance of this battalion on parade bore a striking resemblance to a regiment of the regular army, their arms, accoutrements, and clothing being in an excellent and praiseworthy condition. They went through the manual and platoon exercise, under the command of Major H. E. Irving, perfectly, and afterwards were exercised in battalion drill by Lieutenant-Colonel Skinner in a most satisfactory manner."

On September 29th, the Battalion paraded to receive H. R. H. Prince Arthur and the Governor-General, and furnished guards of honor for both during their stay in the city.

In April, 1870, a general order was published, calling for volunteers for special service in the Red River country, now forming the Province of Manitoba. The quota required from the Thirteenth was eight men, but the number that offered was so great that it was subsequently increased to thirteen. The following non-commissioned officers and men were finally selected : Sergeants James McArthur, John A. Murray and John Emslie ; Corporals John Faulkner and Nathaniel P. Bell ; Privates W. S. Nixon, S. Kilvington, Humphrey Filheahault, James Ayr, Rodney Wetenhall, William Metcalfe, Charles Gilkison, and W. B. Balmer.

The battalion performed its annual drill in a regimental camp at Grimsby, beginning on July 23rd, of which the Adjutant-General made the following favorable report : "The first instance, I believe, of a city battalion performing its annual drill in camp was very successfully carried out by the 13th Battalion, from Hamilton, under the command of Lieut.-Colonel Skinner. This corps marched from Hamilton to Grimsby, a distance of twenty miles, in the latter part of the month of July, moving into camp the same day, remaining under canvas for ten days, and marching back to Hamilton on the tenth day without any casualities, in a manner which reflected great credit on the commanding officer and those under his command."

The Deputy Adjutant General, who inspected the battalion, described it in his report as "a very fine, even-sized body of young men, very steady under arms, move very soldierlike and well."

In 1871, Lieut.-Colonel Skinner organized and commanded the team of Ontario riflemen which went to Wimbledon, on which the Thirteenth had no less than six representatives, Lieut. Little, Color-Sergeant R. Omand, Sergeant F. Sache and Privates George Murison and Joseph Mason. The battalion went into a brigade camp at Niagara on June 6th, 1871, which was composed of 4,795 officers and men. The Thirteenth was commanded by Major Irving, in the absence of Lieut.-Colonel Skinner, who was at Wimbledon. Its strength in camp was twenty-three officers and 389 non-commissioned officers and privates. Lieut. (afterwards Major) J. J. Mason, who acted as supply officer, was specially noticed for zeal and ability in the performance of his duties.

By a general order of May 23rd, 1872, the Dundas and Waterdown companies were detached, and became a part of the 77th Battalion, reducing the strength of the Thirteenth once more to six companies.

A divisional camp for sixteen days was formed at Niagara on June 12th of this year, which consisted of 435 officers and 5,438 non-commissioned officers and privates, divided into three brigades, the second of which was commanded by Lieut.-Colonel Skinner. Captain (afterwards Lieut.-Colonel) A. H. Moore, acted as Brigade Major; Dr. Ryall as Brigade Surgeon. Lieut. (afterwards Major) J. J. Mason, as Supply Officer. Major Irving commanded the Thirteenth during this camp.

The battalion team won the Merchants' Challenge Trophy, and No 2 company the Tait-Brassey Company Cup at the Ontario Rifle Association meeting in 1872, thus auspiciously beginning a long list of successes.

Lieutenant-Colonel Skinner commanded the brigade camp formed at Niagara on June 23rd, 1874, at which Captain A. H. Moore was Brigade Major, and Captain Boice was Supply Officer. The Thirteenth was once more commanded by Major and Brevet Lieutenant-Colonel H. E. Irving.

The battalion again went into camp at Niagara in 1875, as it proved for the last time for many years.

Since 1875 the annual drill has been performed at headquarters, until the summer of the present year, 1899, when the battalion went into camp for three days (June 30th to July 2nd), under command of Lieut.-Col. Henry McLaren.

Lieut.-Colonel Skinner commanded the Infantry Brigade at the review at Toronto in 1879, when the Thirteenth mustered 273 of all ranks.

In 1880, Lieut.-Colonel Gibson had the well deserved honor of being selected to command the Wimbledon team, on which the Thirteenth was represented by eight men. The team succeeded in winning that coveted trophy, the Kolapore Cup.

On the 24th of May, 1884, the Battalion entertained the Royal Grenadiers of Toronto, and both battalions were reviewed in Dundurn Park. The visit of the Grenadiers was returned on Dominion Day, when a volunteer force of more than 4,000 men paraded in Toronto, composed of the Governor-General's Body Guards, the Hamilton, Toronto, and Welland Field Batteries, Governor-General's Foot Guards, Queen's Own Rifles, 6th, 7th, 10th, 12th, 13th, 14th, 34th, 36th and 77th Battalions.

By a general order, dated April 24th, 1885, when the excitement created by the Northwest Rebellion was at its height, two companies were added to the establishment of the battalion. When inspected on June 24th, 341 of all ranks were present. The Battalion was very anxious for active service at the front, but in this they were doomed to disappointment.

The Battalion sustained a serious loss by the burning of the old drill shed on May 23rd, 1886, when the whole of its arms, stores, and band music was consumed. The colors were saved, and many of the trophies of the battalion, which were fortunately stored elsewhere. The loss to the battalion was estimated at $4,000, and that of the Government at $20,000.

On August 28th, 1885, Lieut.-Colonel Skinner retired from the battalion after thirty-one years service, during twenty of which he held command. During his connection with the force Lieutenant-Colonel Skinner had done much to promote the volunteer movement, and especially to encourage rifle practice. He was one of founders of the Ontario Rifle Association, and had commanded the team sent by it to the first Dominion Rifle match at Laprairie. The team from Ontario, that went to Wimbledon in 1872, was chiefly organized by his exertions, and he was deservedly selected to command it. This was the first team of riflemen that had represented any British colony at Wimbledon, and thus the honor of making the Wimbledon meeting a genuinely Imperial event may be said to be due, in the main, to him. He was succeeded by Lieut.-Colonel the Hon. John Morison Gibson.

Lieutenant-Colonel Gibson had won deserved distinction in many ways in civil life. When he graduated from Toronto University in 1863, he had carried off the Prince's Prize, Silver Medals in Classics and Modern Languages and a prize in Oriental Languages. After being called to the Bar in 1867, he entered the law course of the University, and was granted the degree of L. L. B. in 1869, at the same time winning the gold medal. After commencing the practice of law in Hamilton, he soon secured a leading position at the bar of the Province. He had been a Senator of Toronto University since 1873. For five years he had been President of the Hamilton School of Art, which he was instrumental in founding. Since 1879 he had represented the city in the Provincial Legislature, and in 1889 entered the Cabinet as Provincial Secretary. His connection with the volunteer force dated from 1860, and he had been present with the battalion at Ridgeway in 1866. For three years he had been President of the Ontario Rifle Association, and in 1893 he was elected President of the Dominion Rifle Association, an office which he still worthily holds.

The new commanding officer, besides being himself a marksman of the foremost rank, was endowed with almost unlimited zeal and energy. He threw himself heartily into the work of command with the best results. The old Canada Life Assurance Buildings were secured as a drill hall, and when the battalion was inspected on December 30th, 355 of all ranks answered to their names.

Twenty-five thousand dollars were placed in the estimates in 1887 for the construction of a new drill shed, and work was begun upon it during the year. It was finished during 1888 at a cost of nearly $50,000, was occupied on the 14th of September, and formally opened by a most successful concert on October 17th, which was attended by over 1,500 persons. The battalion is now housed in this modern armory, with comfortable quarters for the officers, and rooms for the different companies and the band.

Lieut.-Colonel Gibson, ever anxious to encourage proficiency in the use of the rifle, ordered a number of Morris tubes for the battalion in the autumn of that year.

The adoption of a plan by which the whole of the drill-pay was funded for the benefit of the battalion, early in 1889, produced the most beneficial results. A considerable number of men took their discharge in consequence of the change, but their places were immediately filled with the most desirable class of recruits.

For the first time the Thirteenth took part in the Thanksgiving Day field manœuvres at Toronto on November 7th, 1889, mustering 393 of all ranks.

At the Thanksgiving manœuvres at Toronto on November 6th, 1890, the Thirteenth turned out 400 of all ranks, under Lieut.-Colonel Moore, forming the attacking force in conjunction with C Company, Royal Regiment Canadian Infantry and the Royal Grenadiers, under Lieut.-Colonel Gibson as Brigadier.

On May 24th, 1891, the battalion visited Berlin. This visit aroused much enthusiasm among the officers and men, as it was the first time that the battalion had left the city on the Queen's Birthday for some years. On Saturday afternoon, the 22nd inst., the regiment, under command of Lieut.-Colonel Gibson, paraded at the "Gore" 445 strong, proceeding from thence to the depot and entraining for the trip. Upon arriving at Berlin the corps marched to the Exhibition grounds, where ample accommodation was provided in one of the large frame buildings. After depositing their arms and accoutrements the men were marched to the hotels for dinner. A pleasing feature of the first evening in Berlin was the concert given by the bands of the 13th and 29th Battalions. A splendid programme was rendered, giving much enjoyment to all present. The church parade on the following Sunday was a most imposing ceremony. It was what is termed a "field service." The battalion formed three sides of a hollow square, with the band in the centre and the bugle band on the right flank of the opening. The Rev. A. G. Forneret, using the regulation pulpit of stacked drums, conducted the service. Monday's celebration was a "red letter" day for Berlin. Every train brought crowds of visitors, and before the day was far advanced the streets were thronged with the holiday makers. All along the route of the procession the sidewalks and every possible point of vantage were occupied, cheer after cheer greeting the boys as they marched past. On arrival at the market place the "feu-de-joi" and royal salute were given. In the afternoon the battalion proceeded to the Athletic grounds, where different manœuvres were gone through, followed by a programme of sports, confined to the men of the battalions, under the direction of Lieut.-Colonel Gibson. The band concert was again enthusiastically received. At the conclusion of the concert the battalion paraded, embarking on the train for Hamilton, where they arrived about 2 o'clock the next morning, and were dismissed at the drill hall. Everyone concurred in the opinion that they had spent a most enjoyable time, and could not have been better used by the people of Berlin.

On the Queen's Birthday, 1892, the Thirteenth mustering 417 of all ranks, visited Toronto as the guests of the 48th Highlanders, and were reviewed by the Governor-General, Lord Stanley. A most enthusiastic welcome was given them by the people of Toronto, and one of the most pleasant of the Battalion's trips was the result.

In the year 1889, Lieut.-Colonel (then Major) McLaren suggested that company competitions should be started, and a shield and money prizes be given to the three companies obtaining the highest marks during the whole season's drill. At an earlier period a similar system had been applied by Lieut.-Colonel Irwin, of the Canadian Artillery, to the field batteries under his command. Major McLaren's suggestion was approved of, and with slight variations as to conditions, was carried out until the close of 1895.

Marks were divided as follows :

1.	Armouries, condition of arms, accoutrements, stores and books		100
2.	Class Firing (a) attendance	100	
	(b) scoring company's average	50	150
3.	Attendance at drills		350
4.	Clothing and accoutrements		50
5.	Drill competitions		600
6.	Written examinations (a) officers	75	
	(b) non-commissioned officers	75	150
7.	Field day		100
			1,500

NOTE.—60 per cent. of marks must be obtained to entitle to a prize.

The first competition for general efficiency was won in 1889 by A Company, in 1890 by D Company, in 1891 by B Company, in 1892 by A Company, in 1893 by A Company, in 1894 by A Company, and in 1895 by B Company.

There is no question but that this series of competitions did much to increase the general efficiency of the corps, and perhaps more especially of the non-commissioned officers, who had more work assigned to them than previously, and consequently took a keener interest in their companies, and more especially in their own particular sections. The Battalion efficiency competitions having, in the meantime, been introduced, it was thought better to drop the company competitions for the time being at least, and devote all available energy to the former.

To Lieut.-Colonel Otter belongs the credit of introducing this system into the infantry battalions of No. 2 Military District. In the year 1891 he induced the late Sir Casimir Gzowski, that great friend of the Canadian Militia, to offer a challenge cup to be competed for by the city corps in No. 2 District. The competition during the first year was based largely on a battalion figure of merit.

Major-General Herbert approved so highly of Lieut.-Colonel Otter's idea that he introduced it into other districts, and ultimately applied it to the whole militia force; changing, however, the system of working, and basing it entirely on a company figure of merit his theory being that too much attention had been paid to battalion and brigade drill, to the neglect of squad and company drill. During the last few years, however, marks have been added for battalion drill under the commanding officer, and this, no doubt, is the happy medium, and takes all points into consideration.

Later on another "Gzowski cup" was given to be competed for by the rural corps in No. 2 District. Prominent men in other districts also came forward and imitated Sir Casimir's example so that now most districts have "an efficiency cup" to compete for.

Major-General Hutton takes rather an opposite view of matters from General Herbert, thinking that too much time is devoted to squad and company drill, and that the Canadian militia should push forward into brigade drill and field manœuvres. There is no doubt, however, that the last eight years work, which has been principally squad and company drill, now places the militia force in a better position to appreciate these higher and more extended movements than it would otherwise have been. The general standard of efficiency among non-commissioned officers has, without doubt, been greatly elevated by these battalion competitions.

From lack of time, owing to more extended work, it was found necessary to drop the efficiency competitions during the present drill season, and it is doubtful whether they will be continued again in their present form.

GZOWSKI CUP
FOR
GENERAL EFFICIENCY

During the eight years that efficiency competitions have been held among the city corps of No. 2 District, the "Gzowski Cup" has been won five times by the Thirteenth Battalion, and three times by the Queen's Own Rifles. As the latter, however, won it in 1898, they now have possession of the coveted prize. Whether there will be weeping or rejoicing if these competitions are finally abolished, is a matter of opinion. There is no doubt that all concerned have felt it a terrible grind at times, and that an amount of polishing and cleaning has been done that could not otherwise have been accomplished. There is also no doubt that these competitions have done a great deal towards bringing the regiment up to its present standard, and have been particularly valuable in developing efficiency and responsibility among the ranks of the non-commissioned officers, a most desirable thing to accomplish.

Following is a table showing the scores made by the different city battalions each year in competition for the " Gzowski Cup " :

	1891	1892	1893	1894	1895	1896	1897	1898
2nd Queen's Own Rifles, Toronto	*755	91½	*107.	125	101.43½	143.45	133.97	*150.06
10th Royal Grenadiers. Toronto	645	76	83	96.21	88.20½	138.59	120.39½	147.30
13th Battalion of Infantry, Hamilton	742	*98½	108½	*125 25	*115.62½	*144.84	*137.16	141.00
38th Dufferin Rifles, Brantford	593	55½	55½	60 88	62.94½	132.06	107.98	110.39
48th Highlanders, Toronto	....	70½	90½	102.13	99.84½	104.10	120.77	125.55

* Winner.

On May 24th, 1893, the Forty-Eighth Highlanders returned the visit of the Thirteenth. Unusual good fortune in the matter of weather attended their visit to Hamilton. It was neither too warm nor too cold, and although at times the sky was somewhat overcast, no rain fell. The city presented a busy appearance as thousands of people who, failing some special local attraction, would have probably have gone on some of the many excursions, stayed, with the knowledge that they could have "just as good a time" in Hamilton, on account of the extensive programme furnished by the Thirteenth.

At 10.40 on the morning of the 24th, the visiting battalion arrived and were escorted to the Drill Hall by the Thirteenth. The grand street parade of the day commenced at 11.25, and all along the line vociferous cheers greeted both regiments. The Highlanders were under command of Lieut.-Colonel Davidson, with Majors Cosby and McDonald as field officers.

Dundurn park was not reached until a few minutes after noon. After firing the "feu-de-joie," the two battalions partook of a substantial luncheon served to them at the grounds.

Shortly after 2 o'clock the Brigade, under Lieut.-Colonel Gibson, entered the ball grounds, and as each company passed the saluting point, where the staff was assembled, cheer after cheer greeted them, on account of the soldier-like appearance and steady bearing of every man. The trooping of the colour, physical drill and bayonet exercise as presented by the Thirteenth was beyond criticism. Some of the crack dancers of the Forty-Eighth, accompanied by the bag-pipes, furnished some excellent dancing.

The band concert and fireworks in the evening were witnessed by large crowds who pronounced both items excellent in every respect. At 11.10 the Highlanders paraded at the depot, and, in taking their departure, expressed themselves as more than satisfied with the good time they had and the treatment accorded them by the citizens.

At the Thanksgiving manœuvres at Toronto in this year, the Thirteenth paraded 440 of all ranks, under Lieut.-Colonel Moore, and with the Royal Grenadiers and Forty-Eighth Highlanders formed the attacking force in the sham battle, under command of Lieut.-Colonel Gibson.

At the annual muster and inspection, 460 of all ranks were present, or ninety-two in excess of the establishment.

On the Queen's Birthday, 1894, the Thirteenth, under command of Lieut.-Colonel Moore, visited Galt. The morning was a fine one, and at about eight o'clock on the morning of the 24th, the battalion paraded at the drill hall 500 strong, in review order. The turnout, which is spoken of as being the largest of that season, was most gratifying to all. To quote from a newspaper report of the day, "Too much credit cannot be given to the Hamilton red-coats for their fine appearance, soldierly bearing, and large parade." The journey by train was rather tedious owing to several delays on the road, but the general good humor pervading all ranks was in nowise marred by this cause. On the arrival at Galt the regiment was met by a deputation of the Foresters, under whose auspices the celebration was held. The battalion formed on Water Street, and marched to the Town Hall, where they were dismissed for the purpose of partaking of dinner, which was served for the rank and file in the Skating Rink, the officers being quartered at the different hotels. The 10th Royal Grenadiers, of Toronto, who were also taking part in the celebration, had arrived some time before the Thirteenth. After dinner the parade formed for the purpose of proceeding to the Fair grounds, where a very attractive programme of sports had been arranged for, but the weather, which had been threatening for some time, now declared itself in a steady downpour of rain. It was decided, in consequence, to curtail the proceedings by limiting them to the different manœuvres and exercises of the two regiments. The first item on the programme was the "march past," to the music of the brigade bands. This was splendidly done, and elicited vigorous applause from the spectators. Exhibitions of physical drill and bayonet exercise by squads from the Thirteenth followed, and as the rain showed no signs of abating, the remainder of the programme was cancelled, and a return to the town ordered. A concert by the combined bands of the Thirteenth and Grenadiers had been announced for the evening, and great disappointment was felt when it was found necessary to cancel it on account of several of the instruments having been rendered temporarily useless by the rain. A kindly hospitality was extended on all sides to the members of both corps, and, apart from the wetting received, reminiscences of the trip can not be otherwise than pleasant. The regiment entrained for the return journey at 10.30, arriving in Hamilton shortly before 12 o'clock. In dismissing the men, Colonel Moore thanked them for the good conduct they had observed throughout the day, and expressed his pleasure in having been able to assume command of the battalion on the largest parade in its history.

On Nov. 22nd, the battalion again took part in the Thanksgiving manœuvres at Toronto, numbering 428, of all ranks, under Major Henry McLaren, Lieut.-Colonel Gibson having leave of absence, and Lieut.-Col. Moore being ill.

The battalion, in 1894, was again awarded the Gzowski Cup for general efficiency. The following extract from Major-General Herbert's report will serve to indicate that this distinction was well earned :

"The Thirteenth Battalion was inspected by the Deputy Adjutant-General on Oct. 31st and Nov. 7th by companies. Drill, arms, etc., very good. Answers to questions, excellent. Took part in a field-day at Toronto (paying its own transport), at which advance-guards and the attack were practised, afterwards inspected by the Major-General commanding. The battalion is in excellent order and very enthusiastic ; complete in officers, and over strength in men. In this corps a most efficient system of target practice exists."

On the 26th of December, 1894, the late commanding officer, Lieut.-Colonel Skinner was buried with military honors, the battalion assembling in strength.

The marked success which attended the trip to Galt, naturally elicited an almost unanimous assent on the part of the officers, when invited to attend the demonstrations to be held on the following Queen's Birthday at London. The battalion, in command of Colonel Gibson, paraded at the Drill Hall at 5.45 on the evening of the 23rd, and proceeded in heavy marching order to the T. H. & B. Station. Large crowds gathered there, many with the desire of seeing the first passenger train run on the new road, as well as getting a glimpse of the regiment entraining. On arriving at London, the corps was received by the assembled corps, consisting of No. 1 Company Royal Canadian Infantry, Seventh Battalion of London, "A" Troops of the London Hussars, London Field Battery, and the 38th Dufferin Rifles of Brantford.

The Thirteenth were apportioned most comfortable quarters in the main Exhibition building. The proceedings opened with a review of the brigade, which mustered, all told, 2000. Lieut.-Colonel the Hon. J. M. Gibson was the Brigadier in command. It may be mentioned with a certain amount of pride that out of the total of 2000 the Thirteenth contributed over a quarter, having that day a parade state of 504 officers and men.

The firing of the "feu-de-joie" by the infantry and rifle battalions elicited unbounded admiration and applause from the spectators, on account of the regularity with which it was discharged.

In the march past the Thirteenth were awarded the decision on every point. Seldom had the citizens of London or their visiting friends heard such music as that furnished by the band, headed by Bandmaster Robinson, and as the regiment marched past with every company in perfect line, betraying careful training on the part of the officers, and equal attention on that of the men, they presented an inspiring sight, and cheer after cheer greeted their efforts. The trooping of the colour by the battalion was an event of the day.

The military tournament following was not the least important part of the day's programme, and the members of the Thirteenth, who participated, acquitted themselves most creditably, carrying off a good proportion of the events. The band concert in the evening, followed by the spectacular representation of the seige of " Tel-El-Kebir " afforded much pleasure to all, and brought the celebration to a close.

A complimentary banquet was tendered by the citizens to the officers of the visiting and the local military corps, and in replying to a toast Colonel Gibson thanked Colonel Lindsay, the 7th Fusiliers, and the citizens generally for the kindness shown to the Thirteenth during the day, and extended an invitation to Colonel Lindsay and his battalion to visit Hamilton at an early date.

On November 8th, 1895, Lieut.-Colonel Gibson, having completed thirty-five years service as a volunteer, and thirty-three in the Thirteenth, retired from the command, but " in view of Lieut.-Colonel Gibson's long and faithful service in the militia," the general order added, " and in recognition of his zealous efforts in promoting and encouraging rifle shooting in the force, that officer is permitted to retain his rank as honorary Lieutenant-Colonel of this battalion." By a subsequent general order of March 4th, 1899, Lieut.-Colonel Gibson was appointed an honorary aide-de-camp to the Governor-General, the Earl of Aberdeen.

He was succeeded in command by Lieut.-Colonel Alexander Huggins Moore, a very able and energetic officer, to whose activity while acting as Adjutant, and skilful management of its finances for many years, the battalion owed much of its efficiency.

Lieut.-Colonel Moore had graduated from the Military School during Colonel Peacocke's period of command, and had seen varied and arduous service on the frontier in 1866. On several occasions, as already noticed, he had been selected to act as Brigade Major at successive camps of instruction. In 1876 he had been attached to the School of Gunnery, taking a first-class certificate in gunnery, and in the course of the same year was offered, and declined, an Inspectorship in the North West Mounted Police. He became Brevet Major in 1875, and had been a major in the battalion since 1883.

When one considers the fact that the winning of the " Queen's Prize " at Bisley means that the successful competitor must prove himself the best marksman from a picked 2,000 men, a fair realization of the skill required for such a performance will be obtained. The honor of winning this much coveted trophy for 1895 fell to Canada, and more particularly to Hamilton, Private Hayhurst, of the Thirteenth Battalion, outshooting all his opponents and thereby winning everlasting fame for himself, his corps and Canada. Hayhurst was born in Kendal, Westmoreland, England, in 1868, came out to this country, and eventually settled in Hamilton in 1893, joining E Company of the Thirteenth Battalion on June 9th of the same year. It is therefore but natural that Canada should claim the honor of his

Corporal John Leith and Private W. Richmond, were selected to represent the battalion on the Jubilee contingent which went to England on the occasion of the celebration of the sixtieth year of Her Majesty's reign.

The trips taken by the battalion on the Queen's Birthdays of former years had always been characterised by the fact that the corps was going somewhere where they were, at least, not entire strangers, on account of the comparatively short distances that separated the towns they had visited from Hamilton. Kingston, however, being a considerable distance, and, at the same time, essentially a military town, extra preparations were made to have the the battalion at its best in every possible way on its trip to that city in 1897. With a parade state of 510, the corps entrained at 10 o'clock on the night of Saturday, the 22nd, arriving in Kingston the following Sunday morning about 5 o'clock. One hour later the troops were all detrained and proceeded to the fair grounds, where, under the direction of Major Mason, seventy-five large tents and three marquees had been erected for their accommodation. That day probably the largest church parade ever witnessed in Kingston took place. The Brigade consisted of exactly 1,200 officers and men. The Brigade Review held on Monday, the 24th, Lieut.-Col. Cotton in command, was successful in every re-

THIRTEENTH BATTALION REPRESENTATIVES TO HER MAJESTY'S DIAMOND JUBILEE.

spect. The Brigade line was as follows : "A" Field Battery on the right, the Thirteenth and Fifteenth Battalions in the centre, and the 14th Prince of Wales' Own Rifles on the left. After the " feu-de-joie " and three cheers for Her Majesty, column was formed for the march past, in which the Thirteenth acquitted itself most creditably. The trooping of the colour by the Thirteenth was a new feature to most of the Kingstonians, as only red-coated regiments are privileged to perform this ceremony, and the local regiment is a blue-coated one. The applause that followed it was deafening. After a parade through the town the regiments were dismissed, the Thirteenth assembling at the station at 9.45, all entraining for home in good order. Lieut.-Colonel Cotton, Brigade officer of the day, said that he was proud of temporarily commanding a brigade in which the Thirteenth formed a part. The officers and men of the battalion received unbounded kindness during their visit, more especially from the members of the Prince of Wales' Own Rifles, who were unremitting in their endeavors to make it a pleasant one.

During 1897 an ambulance corps was formed, and the battalion was re-armed with Lee-Enfield rifles.

Lieut.-Colonel Moore retired on November 20th, 1897, and was succeeded by Lieut.-Colonel Henry McLaren, who, during twenty-eight years connection with the battalion, had served in every capacity, from ensign up. Before joining the Thirteenth he had served as a private in the University company of the Queen's Own Rifles, and was one of a detachment from that company drafted into service in the Western Administrative Battalion, in the autumn of 1865. The company formed from the Queen's Own was stationed during the winter of 1865-6 at Sarnia, in anticipation of a Fenian Raid. In 1866 Mr. McLaren joined the home guard, in Hamilton, and three years later he was gazetted an ensign in the Thirteenth. He immediately qualified by taking a second-class certificate at the Military School, and obtained a first-class certificate the following year. In 1883 he performed the duties of Brigade Major at the camp of instruction at Niagara. He obtained a first-class certificate from the Toronto School of Infantry in 1887, and followed this up by taking a long course at Kingston in 1889.

The Thirteenth Battalion, with a parade state of three hundred and sixty-five officers and men, participated in the Thanksgiving field day at Toronto, on November 25th of this year.

Some dissatisfaction having been expressed by the people of Hamilton that the Thirteenth should leave the city on the holiday, it was decided that for the Queen's Birthday of 1898 the corps would remain in town, and contribute to the public celebrations. The Royal Grenadiers, of Toronto, " A " Company of the Seventy-Seventh Battalion, of Dundas, and the Royal Canadian Dragoons, were the invited guests of the day. A grand review of the troops and a sham battle was planned for the forenoon, to be followed in the afternoon with an exhibition by the Dragoons and manoeuvres and exercises by the troops, all under the auspices of the St. George's Society. The Thirteenth Battalion and the Fourth Field Battery paraded at the Drill Hall at 9.15 on the morning of the Queen's Birthday, where they were joined by the Dundas company of the Seventy-Seventh Battalion. On the arrival at the Jockey Club grounds the forces were divided in the following manner : The Thirteenth and the right section of the battery, under Lieut.-Colonel McLaren, formed the attacking force, and the Grenadiers, assisted by the middle and left sections of the battery, the defending force, under Lieut.-Colonel Mason. From a military standpoint the battle was

68

a perfect success, but some of the spectators expressed disappointment, as it did not last long enough, and was perhaps not quite up to their expectations in the way of noise and excitement. In the afternoon performance the hit of the day was made by the Dragoons, who went through many interesting and entertaining tactics. Physical drill by the Grenadiers, the trooping of the colour by the Thirteenth, and march past by the assembled troops, brought the day's proceedings to a close. In the evening the band concert and exhibition of drill by the Dragoons at Dundurn Park was a most enjoyable feature. At 9.45 the combined bands struck up the national anthem, winding up the celebrations at an early hour, by the desire of the committee.

A number of Maxim guns were purchased by the Canadian Government in 1897, and were given to certain of the city corps. The corps receiving them were required to qualify one officer and one non-commissioned officer in the use of the new gun. The Thirteenth Battalion was the first corps to receive a Maxim, and now has a very efficient detachment commanded by Lieut. John D. Laidlaw. The Maxim is the latest type of machine gun adopted by the British Government, and is doubtless the best and most accurate of these

THE MAXIM GUN AND THE GUN DETACHMENT,
THIRTEENTH BATTALION OF INFANTRY.

death-dealing instruments. The gun fires, at its greatest speed, 600 shots per minute, through a single barrel. This barrel passes through a casing filled with water to keep the barrel cool. The water in the casing boils in about one and a half minutes, and the arrangements for the escape of steam and constant supply of water are all provided for in the most complete manner. The work of these guns during Lord Kitchener's recent campaign in the Soudan shows their terrible effectiveness.

The Thanksgiving manœuvres in Toronto were attended again in 1898 by 358 of all ranks.

A pressing invitation having been received from the officers of the Nineteenth Battalion of St. Catharines, it was decided to take the Thirteenth to that town to assist in the local celebration of the Queen's Birthday of 1899. About

69

8.15 on the morning of the 24th, the Battalion paraded at the Drill Hall, showing a parade state of 464 of all ranks. In honor of the day in Hamilton, the regiment was marched to the "Gore," for the purpose of firing a "feu-de-joie," giving a royal salute, and three cheers for the Queen. The entraining at the Stuart St. depot was satisfactorily accomplished, all arriving at St. Catharines in good order at about 11.45. The regiment was escorted by the Nineteenth Battalion Band to "Montebello Park," where, after piling their arms, the companies were marched to the different hotels to partake of dinner. At about 2 p. m., the Brigade, which consisted of the Thirteenth and Nineteenth Battalions, "A" Squadron, Second Dragoons, and two guns of the Welland Field Battery formed up in Montebello Park, proceeding from there to the fair grounds. A royal salute of twenty-one guns by the Battery, followed with a feu-de-joie by the Thirteenth and Nineteenth Battalions, opened the days proceedings. The brigade "march past" in column and quarter column was exceedingly well done and loudly applauded by the spectators. The trooping of the colour and physical drill, as performed by the Thirteenth, were notable features of the day. On conclusion of the programme, the brigade formed for the return march, the Thirteenth depositing their helmets and arms in the train on the way. In the evening a combined concert of the Thirteenth and Nineteenth bands took place. Nearly 2,000 people attended, and satisfaction was expressed on all sides at the splendid renderings of both bands. The treatment accorded to the members of the Thirteenth by their sister corps was hospitable in the extreme. The battalion entrained for Hamilton shortly after 9 p. m., arriving without any special incident, after having spent what has been termed "one of the pleasantest days in its history."

600 YARDS FIRING POINT
AT NEW RANGES.

The want of a modernly equipped rifle range had been a long-felt one for many years by the officers and men of the Thirteenth, and it was in consequence with feelings of the utmost satisfaction that arrangements were finally concluded for the construction of a new range on a site selected by Musketry Instructor Lieutenant Pain and Assistant Instructor Sergt. Hayhurst. The site was approved of by Colonel Otter, and is, without doubt, one of the finest ranges in the Dominion. The official opening took place on Saturday afternoon, Sept.

CHAPTER VII

THE THIRTEENTH BATTALION BAND

HE patriotic fund committee, on October 6th, 1866, presented the commanding officer the sum of $1,000. and a committee, consisting of Lieut.-Colonel Skinner, Captain Watson, Captain Askin and Lieut. Ritchie, was appointed to take the necessary steps towards organizing a band, such being the disposition which the patriotic fund committee desired to be made of the money. A band was immediately organized and in good working order in a few weeks, and since that time the battalion has always had an efficient band. The first bandmaster was Mr. P. Grossman, who held the position till 1869, when he was succeeded by Mr. George Robinson (late of the band of H. M. Prince Consort's Own Regiment). After one year's service Mr. Robinson retired. Mr. Wm. Blanchard then assumed the leadership, but the position again became vacant, owing to his decease, on January 17th, 1871. Mr. Robinson was then induced to assume his former position as bandmaster, in which capacity he has officiated until the present time. In October of 1873, the instruments becoming worn out, it was decided to replace them, and steps were taken for the purchase of a new set of Besson's manufacture, valued at $1,800. The money for the purchase of these instruments was raised by subscription among the officers and men of the battalion, and in March, 1874, the new instruments were placed in the hands of the bandsmen.

Inasmuch as the battalion itself was organized only four years before 1866, the history of the band dates almost identically with the history of the battalion, and November 1st, of this year, bringing to a close the 30 years of George Robinson's labors as bandmaster, the present is an opportune time in which to review briefly the history of the band and its leader.

Before this is done, however, it must not be forgotten that previous to 1866 there were bands in the city—bands with mercurial memberships and an uncertain hold upon existence. Perhaps the first one of these that merits rec-

73

ognition was the organization known as the Temperance band, brought together in 1851, under the leadership of Peter Grossman. It was the outcome of the great wave of temperance which swept over the country at that time, and was run under the auspices of the temperance societies of the city. When the cold water wave of sentiment receded, this band became disorganized, and a new company of players was formed in 1853, under the name of the City band, Mr. Grossman still being its conductor.

About this time Colonel Booker (afterwards Lieut.-Colonel of the Thirteenth Battalion) was much interested and very enthusiastic in military matters,

THE THIRTEENTH BATTALION BAND

and had an independent artillery corps under his control, their guns having been cast for them in the Great Western car shops, which were then located in Hamilton. The Colonel was as enthusiastic about music as he was about military matters, and through his efforts the old City band became merged into the Hamilton Independent Artillery band. This happened in 1856, and, under this name, Mr. Grossman kept his players together until 1862, when, as is nearly always the case, a re-action set in, and for nearly four years the genealogical line of our present well-known band was almost lost. But not altogether, for enough of the old artillery players were around to form the nucleus of a new organization, and that new organization was our own Thirteenth Battalion Band, it being recognized for the first time as a band of the regiment on Nov. 12, 1866, with Mr. Grossman at its head.

It was in 1862, at the time of the Trent trouble, that George Robinson came to Canada and Hamilton with the Rifle Brigade. Although he stayed in the Rifle Brigade for four years, being stationed at Kingston, Montreal and Quebec, he could not forget Hamilton. So much did he think of her and her prospects that he secured his discharge from the Rifles, and in 1866 came back to the city of his choice, little dreaming at the time that he would here be leader of the crack band of the Dominion for a period of thirty years.

At the time Mr. Robinson took charge of the band the state of music in Canada, and in fact, all over America, was not very encouraging. There were good bands and good bandmasters of the old schools, but methods and instruments were of necessity primitive, and the standard of musical composition in use was low. The appearance in Canada of the British military bands did much to cause an improvement in this country, and across the line the day of real advancement may be said to have dawned at the time of the Boston Jubilee festival. George Robinson was not behind in grasping all improvements within reach, and, so far as lay within the often limited means of the band, new instruments were purchased, and a better class of music taken up. The old German instruments of other days were laid away, and Besson's English make substituted. New instruments have made their appearance, and, whenever possible, these were added. Among these are the bass and tenor clarionettes, the oboe, the double bass and slide trombone, the bassoon, French horns, saxaphones and tympani, these latter being among the last added.

Because advantage was taken of these improvements in instruments, and because at all times better things were sought for in the way of compositions, the Band of the Thirteenth Battalion grew in favor, and its fame as a first-class musical organization spread throughout the country. It was not only in and around Hamilton that the bandsmen's services were demanded by the people, but in other Canadian cities also. In Toronto in 1874, at Montreal in 1878 and at Ingersoll in 1879 there were band competitions in which the Hamilton band took part, and under George Robinson's leadership creditably acquitted itself in competition with the best military bands of the country. When the Peace Jubilee was held at Berlin in 1871 the band was there, the big attraction of that immense gathering. At Montreal with the Royal Templars; in Toronto more times than can be easily told; at Sarnia to enliven the proceedings of the great tunnel opening, and in many other Canadian towns has the band played.

In the United States the band's greatest conquests have been made in company with the members of St. Bernard Commandery, Knights Templar, of

Chicago. With this commandery, trips have been made to Chicago, St. Louis, Boston, Denver and Washington, the Canadians on every occasion being royally treated and unstintingly praised by both press and people. The St. Bernard Commandery in 1891 made a visit to Hamilton and to the Thirteenth Battalion Band.

At St. Louis the band and its leader were honored in a marked manner by the late P. S. Gilmore, who was in charge of the musical festivities. That gentleman, with his wide knowledge of bands and band music, selected the Canadian organization, from among the many there, to play a separate selection, a thing done by only one other band, and that one Gilmore's own.

At Washington also an incident occurred that was not only unique, but interesting, and called forth most kindly expressions from the American press. The bandsmen, together, visited the tomb of the great Washington, at Mount Vernon, and there, with the Union Jack draped over the bass drum, played a funeral dirge to the memory of that great man.

During its Denver trip, in 1892, the band went up Pike's Peak, where they played "God Save the Queen." While in Denver the band gave a complimentary concert to the Canadian Maple Leaf Club of Denver. A number of national airs were played, and the large audience was most enthusiastic.

In Chicago the band is well established in the favor of the people, for every time the commandery trips have been taken in past years there have been grand local concerts arranged for, and thousands of Chicago residents have sat, listened to and appreciated the concert numbers of the famous Hamilton organization. The Band accompanied the St. Bernard Commandery to Boston on its visit to that city in 1895. In the parade there were 22,000 Knights and 164 bands, but the Thirteenth Band, as usual, received its full measure of approbation from the spectators.

At various times the band has been engaged by the Grand Trunk Railway to assist at the opening of their different lines. Among other events of this character they were at the openings of the St. Clair Tunnel at Sarnia in 1890 and the new Suspension Bridge over the Niagara River in 1897.

On the occasion of the thirtieth anniversary of Bandmaster Robinson's leadership of the band, November 2nd, 1898, a complimentary benefit concert was tendered him, and an audience of over 2,000 people crowded the Drill Hall. During the evening a gold watch, suitably inscribed with the crest of the corps, was presented to him, a gift from the officers of the corps. The presentation was made by Mrs. McLaren.

CHAPTER VIII

THE WORK OF THE MARKSMEN

A HISTORY of the Thirteenth would be incomplete without a reference, however brief, to the individual shooting of the men who have made the battalion famous for its marksmanship. Thirty-seven years have elapsed since its formation, and it is possible that in our reference to individual marksmen, some may be omitted.

The fathers of the shooting element of the battalion were undoubtedly Capt. Henery, then Adjutant, and Privates Geo. Murison, Donald Nicholson, James Adam, Thomas Freeborn, Joseph Mason and F. Schwartz. For nearly two generations these zealous members of the battalion, encouraged, instructed and assisted the younger shots, and the proud position that the battalion occupies to-day may be traced back to the efforts of these early pioneers in rifle shooting. Through their encouragement and assistance, teams were sent to the first meeting of the Dominion Rifle Association at Laprairie in 1868, and of the Ontario Rifle Association at Toronto in 1869.

These teams included Corp. John Brass, who won Major General Stisted's cup at Toronto, and Corp. J. McArthur, Lieut. J. J. Mason, Privates Wyatt, Rice and Gilkison, as well as Lieuts. Herbert Marsh, John Little (battalion champion 1867) and the Hilton brothers.

The Victoria Rifle Club, of Hamilton, which had its organization about the same time as the Thirteenth, and which was the forerunner of all the rifle clubs in the province, materially encouraged the battalion in its rifle practice.

For many years, Pte. Geo. Murison occupied a prominent place in shooting circles. He won the championship at Laprairie in 1868, and the small-bore championship at Toronto in 1870, and from that time up to his retirement from the battalion his name appears frequently in prominent positions in the prize lists, both of the Dominion and the Ontario Rifle Associations.

Private Jos. Mason had a long and brilliant career as a small-bore shot, year after year either winning the championship or coming within reasonable distance of it. He won the battalion championship in 1879, and, with Private Schwartz, was on the International teams of 1880 and 1882.

Pte. (afterwards Captain) Adam's name also appears with practically equal prominence in the prize lists, in 1868 at Laprairie, and in 1869 at Toronto, while in 1873 he won the small-bore championship in the latter com-

77

petition.   He was also champion shot of the Thirteenth in 1869, 1875 and 1877, and won the small-bore championship at Creedmoor, New York.   For many years his name appears in the prize lists at the D. R. A. and O. R. A. matches.

In 1869 and 1870 the famous Mitchell brothers first appeared upon the scene. John, David and William, and, subsequently, Thomas, Coulson and George. The latter, though hardly able to hold a rifle, won the Turner Cup when a bugler in No. 1 Company. David Mitchell won the battalion championship in 1872, 1874, 1880, 1884, 1886 and 1891, a record not equalled by any other member of the battalion. In addition to this, he has been on the Wimbledon and Bisley teams many times, won the Macdougall Cup at the D. R. A. matches in 1875, has won the Grand Aggregate at Ottawa on more than one occasion, was on the International team of 1882, and in all the prize lists, both at Ottawa and Toronto, has been well to the front.

This may also be said of his brothers, and though, as to three of them, other battalions have now the benefit of their skill Lieut. Mitchell being with the Thirty-second, Captain T. Mitchell with the Twelfth, and Capt. Coulson Mitchell with the Ninetieth yet it is a matter of pride that the shooting qualities of this famous band of brothers originated in the Thirteenth. All have shot brilliantly at times, having won the Governor-General's prize on more than one occasion, but David Mitchell may probably be looked upon as at all times the most reliable member of the sextette, this honor being possibly shared by his brother Thomas. They have always been on the Battalion, Association and Company teams. Lieut. W. Mitchell won the Prince of Wales' prize in 1882, and was on the International team of 1880 ; John won the battalion championship as late as 1894, and Thomas in 1873 and 1876.

Another family of brothers appeared as members of the battalion somewhere about 1868 or 1869 Gilbert, Robert and James Omand and they for many years helped materially in keeping up the shooting record of the battalion besides winning numerous prizes at the meetings of the several rifle associations.

In 1872 the Seventy-seventh Battalion was formed, and the Thirteenth lost such good shots as Ashbury, English, (battalion champion 1868) and Easterbrook, who had done well as members of No. 8 Company of the Thirteenth.

In 1872 two well known names, amongst others, represented the Thirteenth in the battalion matches at Toronto Colonel Gibson and Lieut. Pain. Colonel Gibson had practised regularly and assiduously, and, in that year commenced a career that was almost phenomenal, both with respect to military as well as small-bore rifle shooting. For fifteen years his name appears as a member of the battalion team, and in the meantime he won many first prizes, including the Prince of Wales' prize, at Wimbledon, in 1879, with a record score for the Snider rifle. He, on more than one occasion, won the small-bore championship at Toronto, and he was also a member of the International Team of 1880.

Lieut. Pain, the present efficient Musketry Instructor of the battalion, has also distinguished himself at home and abroad, both with the military and match rifle. He has been on the teams of the Thirteenth for many years, won the battalion championship in 1878, and was a member of both International teams. His services to the battalion, and to the Canadian Military Rifle League, of which he is Secretary, have been invaluable.

Major Mason, who has been Secretary of the Thirteenth Battalion Rifle Association from its organization up to the present time, and who was present at the first meeting of the Dominion Rifle Association at Laprairie, and the Ontario Rifle Association at Toronto, has also contributed to the success of the Thirteenth teams, both by his own shooting and by assistance rendered by him to other members of the battalion. In 1870 he won the battalion championship, and in 1872 the small-bore championship at Toronto, and for about twenty years was a member of the battalion teams, both at Toronto and Ottawa. He, with Lt.-Col. Gibson, Capt. Adam and Sgt. D. Mitchell, was for three years a member of the team which, after a keen contest, finally won the London Merchants' Cup at Toronto in 1880, it having to be won three times consecutively before becoming permanent property.

In 1877 Sergt. Henry Marris commenced a brilliant career by winning two first prizes at Toronto. In 1882 he won the three aggregates at Toronto, a feat which, like that of Surgeon-Lieut. Bertram at Bisley, has perhaps never been equalled. He won the battalion championship in 1888 and 1892; in 1891 he won the Carrington Cup at Wimbledon, and on several occasions at Ottawa he occupied high places both in the Governor-General's Match and the Grand Aggregate. He has been many times on the Wimbledon and Bisley teams, and has helped more than once to win the Kolapore Cup.

Lieut. Geo. Margetts came to the front in 1879 and maintained a position on the battalion team until his transfer to the Twenty-fifth Battalion, Elgin. He was on the International team in 1882, was a reliable shot and always ready to assist his brother riflemen in their competions.

In 1881 Major F. B. Ross first distinguished himself by winning the battalion championship, a feat which he repeated in 1883 and 1890.

About this time Sgt. W. M. Goodwin joined the battalion, and was prominently connected with all the teams, both battalion and company, up to the time of his transfer to the Seventh Fusiliers of London. He was a member of the team that assisted in defeating that from the United States in 1882, and was on the Kolapore Cup Team in 1884. In 1887 he won the Elkington Cup at Toronto. He was equally at home with both the match rifle and military weapon.

Two other members of the battalion were of great assistance during this period, Sergt. Oliver Hancock, a well known member of No. 2 Company, and Staff-Sergt. W. H. Clarke, previously a member of the Queen's Own Rifles.

In 1884 Pte. Harry Graham, an enthusiastic rifleman, won the battalion championship, and attended all the prize meetings for some years.

In 1885 the Murdoch brothers—George and Andrew—became proficient shots, and on many an occasion assisted the Thirteenth in winning a victory.

In 1887 the battalion championship was won by Pte. J. R. Adam, a son of Capt. Adam, who gave promise of becoming a brilliant shot, and whose retirement from the battalion, after a short service, was greatly regretted.

In 1889 Major Zealand won the battalion championship, and his name runs concurrently with that of Major Ross through all the prize lists of the D. R. A. for many years.

Of later years one of the most prominent shots of the Thirteenth has been Color-Sergt. Skedden, who has had a marvellous career since his first appearance in 1890, having won numerous prizes at Toronto, Ottawa, Wimbledon and Bisley. He holds the record for tie shooting at Bisley, having had to make eighteen consecutive bulls-eyes in order to win the Daily Graphic Cup; won the Governor-General's gold medal at Ottawa this year (1899); holds battalion championship, and is probably the best all-round shot now in the battalion.

Did space permit, we could give the names of a host of others who, both in the past and in recent years, have by their skill contributed to the successful career of the Thirteenth as a shooting regiment. Amongst them are Col.-Sgt. Thomas Mitchell (battalion championship 1893 and 1898); Sergt. D. Garson (battalion championship 1896); Staff-Sergt. T. H. Hayhurst, G. M., winner of the Prince of Wales' Prize in 1889 and the Queen's in 1897, and was battalion champion in the same year; Sergt. Major Huggins (battalion championship 1896); Lieut. W. L. Ross, who made such a gallant fight for the Queen's Prize in 1897; Sergts. F. S. Morison, C. W. Spencer, W. Will, H. McNeilly, E. R. Marshall and A. Miller, Lieut. R. A. Robertson and Capt. J. H. Herring. Lieut. A. Robertson, now of the Seventy-seventh, was for some years a popular and valuable member of the Thirteenth teams.

We must not omit a special reference to Surgeon-Lieut. Bertram, of the Seventy-seventh, whose career at Bisley this year was of a marvellous character, and who most justly won the admiration of all shooting men for his wonderful shooting there. He was originally a member of the Thirteenth, with which battalion he was prominently identified until his transfer to the Seventy-seventh. No man in Canada has won greater honors or carried them more modestly than Surgeon-Lieut. Bertram. He was champion shot of the Thirteenth in 1895.

Such a record as this can scarcely be excelled, and will be undeniably hard to maintain. But whatever emergency the coming years may bring, we may rest assured that with an officer of such recognized ability and energy as Lieut.-Colonel McLaren in command, supported by the present efficient body of officers and non-commissioned officers, it will find the Thirteenth true to its motto, "SEMPER PARATUS."

LIST OF OFFICERS

The Hon. Isaac Buchanan, Lieut.-Col. Nov. 28th, 1862. Retired Dec. 30th, 1864.

† Alfred Booker, Lieut.-Col. Hamilton Field Battery, April 23rd, 1857. Lieut.-Colonel 13th Batt., Jan. 27th, 1865. Retired from command of 13th Batt. Aug. 10th, 1866. Retired, retaining rank as commandant of Hamilton, June 14th, 1867.

† James A. Skinner, joined Highland Co. in 1855, and was Capt. when 13th was organized. Major Dec. 26th, 1862. Lieut.-Col Aug. 10th, 1866. R. R. R. Aug. 27th, 1880.

J. Edwin O'Reilly, Major Dec. 26th, 1862. R. R. R. Feb. 10th, 1865.

† Stephen T. Cattley, Lieut. July 17th, 1861. Major Feb. 24th, 1865. Brevet Lieut.-Col. March 15th, 867. Left limits July 5th, 1867.

† Henry Erskine Irving, Ensign April 10th, 1863. Lieut. May 12th, 1864. Major July 5th, 1867. Brevet Lieut.-Col. July 5th, 1872. R. R. R. Jan. 12th, 1883.

† Alexander H. Askin, Ensign Dec.5,1862. Lieut. March 5th, 1863. Captain Dec. 30th, 1864. Major (Pro.) Oct 22nd, 1869. R. R. R. of Captain Sept. 28th, 1877.

† Isaac Ryall, M. B., Surgeon April 4th, 1866. Surgeon-Major April 6th, 1886. R. R. R. May 3rd, 1889.

John Brown, Captain Nov. 28th, 1862. R. R. R. Sept. 14th, 1866.

John Octavious Macrae, Lieut. Nov. 28th, 1862. Resigned May 12th, 1864.

Peter Toronto Buchanan, Ensign Nov. 28th, 1862. Lieut. July 29th, 1864. Left limits March 2nd, 1866.

George Herve Mingaye, Captain Dec. 5th, 1862. Left limits Dec. 30th, 1864.

John A. Ward, Lieut. Dec. 5th, 1862. Resigned March 5th, 1863.

Donald McInnes, Captain Dec. 5th, 1862. Resigned May 12th, 1864.

George H. Gillespie, Lieut. Dec. 5th, 1862. Capt. March 18th, 1863. Retired Dec. 15th, 1865.

Thomas Bell, Lieut. Dec. 11th, 1862. Resigned April 28th, 1865.

W. F. Biggar, Lieut. Dec. 11th, 1862. Captain April 28th, 1865. Resigned Nov. 10th, 1865.

A. Jamieson, Ensign Dec. 11th, 1862. Lieut. April 28th, 1865. Resigned May 1st, 1866.

John McKeown, Captain Dec. 19th, 1862. Resigned July 10th, 1863.

Maurice O'Connor, Lieut. Dec. 19th, 1862. Resigned July 10th, 1863.

Martin Fitzpatrick, Ensign Dec. 19th, 1862. Resigned July 10th, 1863.

Robert N. Law, Captain Jan. 9th, 1863. R. R. R. Sept. 14th, 1866.

A. S. Wink, Lieut. Jan. 9th, 1863. Resigned April 23rd, 1865.

Wm. Inkson, Ensign Jan. 9th, 1863. Resigned Dec. 29th, 1865.

C. J. Lloyd, Captain and Adjutant, March 5th, 1863. Resigned Dec. 2nd, 1864.

John Stewart Henderson, Captain March 5th, 1863. R. R. R. March 2nd, 1866.

Alexander Turner, Lieut. March 5th, 1863. Resigned July 10th, 1863.

Robert Park, Ensign March 5th, 1863. Lieut. April 28th, 1865. Left limits Dec. 22nd, 1865.

C. Feeley, Ensign March 5th, 1863. Resigned April 10th, 1865.

Maitland Young, Lieut. March 18th, 1863. Resigned 1863.

John Young (Jr.), Ensign March 18th, 1863. Lieut. Dec. 30th, 1864. Resigned Oct. 31st. 1867.

† Frederick Ewing Ritchie, Ensign April 10th, 1863. Lieut. Dec. 30th, 1864. Captain Oct. 26th, 1866. R. R. R. Dec. 3rd, 1869.

Edward Hilton, Lieut. April 10th, 1863. Resigned May 12th, 1864.

† John H. Watson, Ensign Jan. 31st, 1863. Lieut. July 15th, 1864. Capt. May 17th, 1865. Died 1869.

F. M. Atkinson, Lieut. Aug. 12th, 1864. Left limits Dec. 30th, 1864.

George S. Papps, Lieut. Jan. 31st, 1863. Resigned 1865.

† Percy Gore Routh, Ensign Feb. 24th, 1865. Lieut. March 2nd, 1866. Captain Sept. 14th, 1866. R. R. R. Oct. 26th, 1866.

† Joshua John Hebden, Ensign April 28th, 1865. Lieut. Oct. 26th, 1866. Captain Oct. 22nd, 1869. Drill Instructor March 17th, 1870. Acting Adjutant, July 14th, 1870. Died Sept. 1st, 1872.

81

+ Robert Grant, Ensign April 28th, 1865. Lieut. Dec. 22nd, 1865. Captain March 2nd, 1866. Paymaster Oct. 26th, 1866. Hon. Major Oct. 26th, 1871. Died June 29th, 1877.

John Billings, Lieut. April 22nd, 1865. Resigned Dec. 22nd, 1865.

+ Charles Randolph Montgomery Sewell, Ensign April 28th, 1865. Lieut. Dec. 22nd, 1865. R. R. R. Sept. 24th, 1866.

+ J. W. Ferguson, Lieut. April 28th, 1865. Capt. Sept. 14th, 1866. Resigned Dec. 28th, 1866.

+ Alexander William Roy, Ensign May 19th, 1865. Lieut. Oct. 21st, 1867. Captain Nov. 5th, 1869. R. R. R. March 10th 1877.

+ John Henery, Captain and Adjutant Aug. 18th, 1865. R. R. R Aug. 26th, 1870.

+ The Hon. John Morison Gibson, Ensign Dec. 22nd, 1865 Lieut. March 2nd, 1866. Capt. Oct. 26th, 1866 Brevet-Major Oct. 26th, 1871. Bt. Lieut.-Col. Oct. 26th, 1876. Regt. Major Jan. 25th, 1881. Regt. Lieut.-Col. Aug. 27th, 1886. Hon. Lieut.-Col. Nov. 9th, 1898. A. D. C. to H. E. the Gov.-Gen. March 2nd, 1894. Re-appointed A. D. C. March 3rd, 1896.

+ Charles Armstrong, Ensign Dec. 29th, 1865. Lieut. Sept. 14th, 1866. Capt. Dec. 28th, 1866. Hon Major and Paymaster June 14th, 1878. R. R. R Aug. 30th 1897.

+ Hugh C. Baker, Ensign May 1st, 1866. Resigned March 25th, 1870.

+ Joseph M. McKenzie, Ensign June 28th, 1866. Left limits July 24th, 1868.

+ John B. Young, Ensign June 22nd, 1866. Lieut. March 10th, 1867. Captain Dec 3rd, 1869. R. R. R. April 9th, 1875.

+ John J. Mason, Quarter Master and Ensign June 22nd, 1866. Lieut. May 3rd, 1867. Hon. Capt June 22nd, 1881. Hon Major June 22nd, 1891. Paymaster Aug. 30th, 1897.

+ Alexander Huggins Moore, Pro. Ensign June 8, 1866. Ensign Sept. 14, 1866. Lieutenant Dec. 28th, 1866. Captain Jan. 26th, 1870. Drill Instructor July 3rd, 1873. Acting Adjutant Feb. 5th, 1874. Brevet Major Jan. 28th, 1875. Adjutant Jan. 13th, 1882. Regt. Major Sep. 28th, 1883. Bt. Lieut.-Col. Jan. 12, 1893. Regt. Lt.-Col. Dec. 21st, 1895. R. O. 10th Nov. 1897.

James John Larkin Boice, Lieut. March 8th, 1867. Captain Sep. 1st, 1872. R. R. R July 21, 1876.

+ Allan Napier McNab Stewart, Ensign Jan. 31st, 1868. Lieut. Oct. 22nd, 1869. Died Feb. 23rd, 1872.

+ Charles D. Cory, Ensign Jan. 31st, 1868. Left limits March 25th, 1870.

George Hope, Ensign Jan. 31, 1868. Resigned Dec. 17, 1869.

+ John Little, Ensign Jan. 31st, 1868. Pro. Lieut. March 25th, 1870. Lieut. May 23rd, 1872. Resigned July 10th, 1874.

Thomas Herbert Marsh, Ensign July 24th, 1868. Lieut. March 25th, 1870. Resigned Feb. 23rd, 1872.

Charles O'Reilly, M.D., Asst. Surgeon Aug. 21st, 1868. Resigned May 13th, 1870.

Edward Francis Caddy, Ensign Nov. 11th, 1869. Lieut. March 22nd, 1872. Capt. July 21st, 1876. R. R. R. Jan. 28th, 1881.

Henry McLaren, Ensign March 4th, 1869. Lieut. Dec. 3rd, 1869. Capt. April 9th, 1875. Brevet Major April 9th, 1885. Regt. Major Aug. 27th, 1886. Lieut.-Col. Dec. 13th, 1897.

Robert Knight Hope, Ensign (pro). Dec. 17th, 1869. Ensign May 9th, 1872. Lieut. June 12th, 1872. R. R. R. Dec. 16th, 1876.

+ Peter Benjamin Barnard, Ensign March 25th, 1870. Lieut. March 22nd, 1872. Captain March 10th, 1877. Brevet Major March 9th, 1887. R. R. R. July 11th, 1890.

Charles Hyla Holden, Ensign March 25th, 1870. Resigned June 7th, 1872.

Charles G. Dyett, Ensign (Pro.) May 13th, 1870. Ensign June 10th, 1871. Resigned Oct. 10th, 1873.

Joseph Macready, Ensign, Adjutant and Drill Instructor June 2nd, 1871. Lieut. March 22nd, 1872. Capt. July 21st, 1876. R. R. R. Dec. 8th, 1881.

Gilbert Wakefield Griffin, Ensign March 22nd, 1872. Lieut. Nov. 22nd, 1873. R. R. R. Sep. 28th, 1877.

James Adam, Ensign March 22nd, 1872. Lieut. July 21st, 1876. Captain Jan. 28th, 1881. R. R. R. May 9th, 1890. Musketry Instructor Oct. 31st, 1890.

Edward Cartwright Kerr, Ensign June 7th, 1872. Lieut. July 21st, 1876. Resigned Dec. 16th, 1876.

Henry Strange, M. D., Asst. Surgeon June 7th, 1872. Resigned Nov. 22nd, 1873.

Daniel Sullivan Murphy, Ensign June 12th, 1872. Lieut. July 10th, 1874. Resigned July 21st, 1876.

+ Robert Crockett, Ensign Nov. 22nd, 1873. Lieut. April 22nd, 1875. Capt June 14th, 1878. R. R. R. June 27th, 1884. Major 33rd Huron Battalion May 22nd, 1891.

+ John Stoneman, Ensign March 13th, 1874. Lieut. Sep. 14th, 1877. Captain Jan. 28th, 1881. Brevet Major Jan 28th, 1891. Regt. Major Jan 24th, 1896.

Edmund Graves Kittson, M. D., Asst. Surgeon June 19th, 1874. Res. Dec. 26th, 1876.

Angus Peter Spohn, Ensign (pro.) May 14th, 1875. Res Jan. 28th, 1876.

+ Alfred Mackeand, Ensign May 28th, 1875. Acting Adjutant Jan. 22nd, 1876. Lieut. Jan. 14th, 1877. R. R. R. Jan. 28th, 1881. Capt. Winnipeg Infantry Co. Lieut. Col. 90th Batt. Rifles, Winnipeg, May 29th, 1885.

Thomas Kilner Mackeand, Ensign July 21st, 1875. Lieut. March 9th, 1877. R. R. R. Jan. 28th, 1881. Capt. No. 4 Co., Chatham, 24th Kent Batt. March 21st, 1890.

Archibald Willard Fergusson, Ensign (Pro). March 9th, 1877. Res. Sep. 28th, 1877.

Joseph Francis Brien, Ensign (Pro). April 6th, 1877. Left limits July 27th, 1877.

John Boultbee, Ensign (Pro). July 27th, 1877. Ensign Nov. 26, 1880. Transferred to 7th Battalion, London.

82

John Franklin Monck, Ensign (Pro). July 27th, 1877. Res. Oct. 30th, 1879.

John Jacques Stuart, Ensign Sep. 28th, 1877. Lieut. May 31st, 1878. Capt. Jan. 13th, 1882. Actg. Adjt. Sep. 14th, 1883. Adjt. April 18th, 1884. Brevet Major Jan. 13th, 1892. Transferred to R. O. Feb. 1st, 1898.

Horace Reginald Ridout, Ensign (Pro). Dec. 22nd, 1877. Res. June 4th, 1880.

Victor Alexander Robertson, Ensign (Pro). May 31st, 1878. Res. Jan. 16th, 1880.

Herbert Spohn Griffin, M. D., Asst. Surgeon Oct. 30th, 1879. Captain Oct. 30th, 1884. Surgeon Major May 3rd, 1889.

Charles Sumner Scott, 2nd Lieut. (Pro). April 9th, 1880. 2nd Lieut. Nov. 26th, 1880. Lieut. Aug. 5th, 1881. Res. June 28th, 1882.

Frederick John Gibson, 2nd Lieut. (Pro). Sept. 3rd, 1880. 2nd Lieut. Nov. 26th, 1880. Lieut. Aug. 5th, 1881. Res. Aug. 31st, 1883.

Robert Bryson Osborne, 2nd Lieut. (Pro). Oct. 8th, 1880. 2nd Lieut. Nov. 26th, 1880. Lieut. Aug. 5th, 1881. Res. Feb. 3rd, 1882. Re-appointed Lieut. Nov. 9th, 1883. R.R. R. June 17th, 1887.

Duncan J. Campbell, 2nd Lieut. (pro.) Aug. 5th, 1881. Res. June 28th, 1882.

Wm. Gilzen Reid, 2nd Lieut. (pro.) Aug 5th, 1881. 2nd Lieut. Oct. 3rd, 1882. Lieut. Dec. 1st, 1882. Capt. April 18th, 1884. R. R. R. April 24th, 1891.

Edward Gibson Zealand, 2nd Lieut. (pro.) May 12th, 1882. 2nd Lieut. Oct. 3rd, 1882. Lieut. Dec. 1st, 1882. Captain June 27th, 1884. Brevet Major Aug. 15th, 1895. Regimental Major Feb. 15th, 1898.

Wm. John Coulson, 2nd Lieut. (pro.) May 12th, 1882. 2nd Lieut. Oct. 3rd, 1882. Lieut. Dec. 1st, 1882. R. R. R. June 18th, 1886.

George McLaren Brown, 2nd Lieut. (pro.) May 12th, 1882. 2nd Lieut. Oct. 3rd, 1882. Lieut. Dec. 1st, 1882. Captain Aug. 27th, 1886. R. R. R. Aug. 29th, 1888.

Edmund Evelyn Wentworth Moore 2nd Lieut. (pro.) July 31st, 1882. 2nd Lieut. Oct. 3rd, 1882. Lieut. Dec. 1st, 1882. Capt. Aug. 27th, 1886. Brevet Major Aug. 27th, 1896.

John Cowan Gillespie, 2nd Lieut. (pro.) Sept. 11th, 1883. 2nd Lieut. Dec. 22nd, 1882. Lieut. April 18th, 1884. Captain June 17th, 1887. R. R. R. of Lieut. April 20th, 1888.

Sidney Chilton Mewburn, 2nd Lieut. (pro.) Aug. 31st, 1883. 2nd Lieut. Sept. 11th, 1883. Lieut. June 27th, 1884. Capt. April 20th, 1888. Brevet Major May 9th, 1898.

John Bradley Patterson, 2nd Lieut. (pro.) Aug. 31st, 1883. Res. June 27th, 1884.

James Wm. Gordon Watson, 2nd Lieut. (pro.) April 18th 1884. 2nd Lieut. Jan. 8th, 1886. Lieut. March 5th, 1886. Capt. Aug. 29th, 1888. R. R. R. of Lieut. March 1st, 1889.

Henry Gardner Marquis, 2nd Lieut. (pro.) June 27th, 1884. Res. March 5th, 1886.

James Walker Hendrie, 2nd Lieut. (pro.) Feb. 6th, 1885. Res. Dec. 23rd, 1887.

Robert Hobson, 2nd Lieut. (pro.) April 10th, 1885. Res. April 29th, 1887.

Frederick Blythe Ross, 2nd Lieut. (pro.) Feb. 6th, 1885. 2nd Lieut. March 31st, 1886. Lieut. June 18th, 1886. Capt. March 1st, 1889. Brevet Major March 1st, 1899.

William Orlando Tidswell, 2nd Lieut. (pro.) April 10th, 1885. 2nd Lieut. March 21st, 1887. Lieut. April 29th, 1887. Capt. May 9th, 1890. Adjutant Feb. 7th, 1898.

Alexander David Stewart, Captain (pro.) April 24th, 1885. Res. Nov 19th, 1886.

Richard John Duggan, Captain (pro.) April 24th, 1885. Res. Aug 27th, 1886.

George Thomas Tuckett, Lieut. (pro.) April 24th, 1885. Res. Feb. 4th, 1886.

Charles Albert Chapman, 2nd Lieut. (pro.) April 24th, 1885. 2nd Lieut. March 30th, 1888. Lieut. May 9th, 1888. Res. July 6th, 1888.

Alexander Duncan Cameron, 2nd Lieut. (pro.) May 15th, 1885. Res. May 3rd, 1889.

John Wm. Bowman, 2nd Lieut. (pro.) June 18th, 1886. 2nd Lieut. Aug. 15th, 1887. Lieut. Oct. 21st, 1887. Capt. July 11th, 1890. R. R. R. of Lieut. Jan. 30th, 1891.

Percy Domville, 2nd Lieut. (pro.) April 7th, 1887. 2nd Lieut. March 30th, 1888. Lieut. May 9th, 1888. Capt. Jan. 30th, 1891. R. R. R. Jan. 12th, 1895. Re-appointed 2nd Lieut. Sept. 29th, 1898.

Albert Edward Carpenter, 2nd Lieut. (pro.) June 17th, 1887. 2nd Lieut. June 30th, 1888. Lieut. Jan. 4th, 1889. Appointed to Infantry School Corps Sept. 16th, 1889.

Wm. Woodburn Osborne, 2nd Lieut. (pro.) Oct. 21st, 1887. 2nd Lieut. Aug. 15th, 1888. Lieut. Jan. 4th, 1889. Capt April 24th, 1891. R. R. R. Oct. 23rd, 1896.

Albert Pain, 2nd Lieut. (pro.) July 6th, 1888. Supernumerary 2nd Lieut. May 20th, 1899.

Henry Blois Witton, 2nd Lieut (pro.) July 6th, 1888. 2nd Lieut. Nov. 30th, 1889. Lieut. Jan. 31st, 1890. R. R. R. Jan. 24th, 1896.

Thomas Hobson, 2nd Lieut. (pro.) July 6th, 1888. Ret. May 22nd, 1891.

Alexander Bryson Osborne, M D., Asst. Surgeon June 14th, 1889. Transferred to Hamilton Field Battery as Surgeon May 22nd, 1891.

George Douglas Fearman, 2nd Lieut. (pro.) Aug. 2nd, 1889. 2nd Lieut. Aug. 15th, 1890. Lieut. Oct. 31st, 1890. Capt. Feb. 7th, 1898.

John Dickson Laidlaw, 2nd Lieut. (pro.) Aug. 2nd, 1889. 2nd Lieut. March 31st, 1891. Lieut. May 22nd, 1891.

John Henry Herring, 2nd Lieut. (pro.) Aug. 2nd, 1889. 2nd Lieut. June 10th, 1890. Lieut. July 11th, 1890. Capt. Jan. 24th, 1896.

Charles Alfred Peterson Powis, 2nd Lieut. (pro.) Aug. 2nd, 1899. 2nd Lieut. June 30th, 1890. Lieut. Sept. 5th, 1890. Capt. Oct. 23rd, 1896.

Walter Hamilton Bruce, 2nd Lieut. (pro.) Aug. 2nd, 1889. 2nd Lieut. Sept. 15th, 1890. Lieut. Oct. 31st, 1890. Capt. Feb. 15th, 1898.

† Robert Hodgetts Labatt, 2nd Lieut. May 1st, 1890. Lieut. May 30th, 1890. Captain Jan. 12th, 1895.

83

Thomas George Margetts, 2nd Lieut. (pro.) Jan. 31st, 1890. Res. Nov. 3rd, 1893.

Peter T. Robertson, 2nd Lieut. (pro.) July 11th, 1890. Left limits Jan. 12th, 1895.

Wm. Alexander Logie. 2nd Lieut. (pro.) Dec. 31st, 1890. 2nd Lieut. Nov. 30th, 1893. Lieut. Jan. 24th, 1896.

James Harvey 2nd Lieut. (pro.) Dec. 31st, 1890. 2nd Lieut. June 30th, 1891. Lieut. July 10th, 1891. Res May 13th, 1892. Re-appointed 2nd Lieut. Sept. 30th, 1892. Res. Oct. 13th, 1893

George Septimus Rennie, M. D., C. M., Asst. Surgeon July 10th, 1891. Hon. Surgeon Capt Sept. 10th, 1896.

Thomas W. Lester, 2nd Lieut. (pro.) Nov. 20th, 1891. 2nd Lieut. June 30th, 1892. Lieut. Aug. 10th, 1892. Hon. Capt. and Quarter Master Sept. 20th, 1898.

Walter Gibb Townsend, 2nd Lieut. (pro.) Nov. 20th, 1891. Res. May 13th, 1892.

Frank Russell Waddell, 2nd Lieut. (pro.) Nov. 20th, 1891. 2nd Lieut. June 30th, 1892. Lieut Jan. 12th, 1895.

Ralph King. 2nd Lieut. (pro.) May 13th, 1892. 2nd Lieut. Aug. 12th, 1894. Lieut. Feb. 8th, 1896.

Charles Garton Barker, 2nd Lieut. (pro.) June 2nd, 1893. 2nd Lieut. Aug. 12th, 1894. Lieut. Oct. 23rd, 1896. Acting Adjutant May 14th, 1897.

Wm. Leaper Ross, 2nd Lieut. (pro.) Nov. 3rd, 1893. 2nd Lieut. June 3rd, 1898.

John Billings, Jr., 2nd Lieut (pro.) June 1st, 1895. Res. Oct. 3rd, 1898.

Wm. Renwick Marshall, 2nd Lieut. (pro.) Oct. 13th, 1893. 2nd Lieut. Aug. 6th, 1895. Lieut. Feb. 7th 1898. Transferred to Second (special service) Battalion Royal Regiment Canadian Infantry for service in South Africa, Oct. 24th, 1899.

Frederick Parsons, 2nd Lieut. (pro.) June 15th, 1895. 2nd Lieut. June 30th, 1896. Lieut. Feb. 15th, 1898. Res. Oct. 18th, 1898.

John Willis Ambrey, 2nd Lieut. (pro.) Feb. 8th, 1896. 2nd Lieut. Aug. 13th, 1898. Res. May 12th, 1899.

Robert Alexander Robertson, 2nd Lieut. (pro.) Feb. 8th, 1896. 2nd Lieut. June 30th, 1896. Lieut. Sept. 29th, 1898.

The Rev. Geo. A. Forneret, Hon. Chaplain, Oct. 17th, 1896.

O Robert Rowley 2nd Lieut. Oct. 23rd, 1896. Transferred from 77th Batt. Res. Oct. 18th, 1898.

Archibald Kerr McLaren, 2nd Lieut. (pro.) Feb. 7th, 1898. 2nd Lieut. March 31st, 1898. Lieut. Oct. 18th, 1898.

Alexander Franklin Zimmerman, 2nd Lieut. (pro.) Feb. 7th, 1898. 2nd Lieut. Aug. 13th, 1898.

Arthur Edward Mason, 2nd Lieut. (pro.) Feb. 15th, 1898. 2nd Lieut. Aug. 13th, 1898.

Gordon John Henderson, 2nd Lieut. Oct. 10th, 1898. Previous service, Capt. 6th Fusiliers, Montreal, May 11th, 1895. Transferred to 13th Batt. Oct. 18th, 1898.

John Alexander Turner, 2nd Lieut. (pro.) Oct. 10th, 1898.

Edward Vaughan Wright, 2nd Lieut. (pro.) May 12th, 1899.

RECORD OF RIFLE SHOOTING

By 13th Battalion of Infantry, from 1863 to 1899 Inclusive

Compiled by Captain J. H. Herring.

Feeling that the collection of our records of rifle shooting, covering as it does a period of over thirty years, into some convenient and compact form would not only be useful to those who take an interest in rifle shooting to-day, but interesting reading to those who have helped to make those records what they are, is my apology for arranging the following pages. If they only act as some slight incentive to others in maintaining the high standard of efficiency which these records show I shall indeed be gratified. I must express my sincere thanks to Major J. J. Mason and Lieut. Albert Pain for invaluable assistance given me in compiling the various competitions to completion, as, without the aid of their ancient secretarial minutes of meetings of the Victoria Rifle Club and Thirteenth Battalion Rifle Association, some of the competitions herein would have been incomplete.

J. HENRY HERRING, Captain,
13th Batt. Infantry.

Record of Winner 13th Infantry First Battalion Prize and Medal.

Date.	Number of Competitors.	NAME.	Score.	Possible.	Date	Number of Competitors.	NAME.	Score.	Possible.
1867		Sgt. Little, No. 6			1884	124	Pte. D. Mitchell	55	75
*1868		Pte. D. English, No. 6			1885	100	Pte. H. Graham	56	75
1869		Pte. James Adam			1886		Pte. D. Mitchell	46	75
1870		Lt. J. Mason			1887		rte. J. R. Adam	57	75
1871		Col. Sgt. Omand, No. 7			1888		Corp. H. Marris	71	105
1872		Pte. D. Mitchell	65	81	1889		Capt. E. Zealand	67	105
1873	70	Pte. T. Mitchell	72	84	1890		Capt. F. B. Ross	62	105
1874	62	Pte. D. Mitchell	69	84	1891		S. Sgt. D. Mitchell	80	105
1875	70	Ensign Jas. Adam	45	60	1892		Sgt. H. Marris	90	105
1876	96	Sgt. Thos. Mitchell	64	75	1893		Pte. Thos. Mitchell	81	105
1877	90	Lt. J. Adam	54	75	1894		Corp. John Mitchell	81	105
1878	80	Sgt A. Pain	50	75	1895		Pte. Thomas A. Bertram	81	105
1879	80	Pte. Jos. Mason	55	75	1896		Sgt. D. Garson	77	105
1880	96	Sgt. D. Mitchell	62	75	1897		S. Sgt. T. H. Hayhurst, G. M.	92	105
1881	70	Pte. F. B. Ross	56	75	1898		Sgt. Thos. Mitchell	94	105
1882	86	Corp. W. L. Goodwin	50	75	1899		Col. Sgt. E. Skedden	93	105
1883	100	S. Sgt. F. B. Ross	61	75	1900				

JUNIORS WHO HAVE BECOME SENIORS EACH YEAR BY WINNING $5.00 OR MORE.

*1868—First O. R. Matches were held this year.
†1869—13th Batt. Infantry affiliated with O. R. Ass., 24th April, 1869.

1870—Lt. Mason; Sgts. Omand and Brass; Corpls. Dunnett and Sache; Ptes. Arnold, Crocker, Mooney, W. Mitchell.
1871—Ptes. Jas. Adam, T. Willis, Shearer, Creig and Hamilton.
1872—Corp. Laing; Ptes. James Omand, Jos. Mason, Leitch, G. Murison, Perkiss.
1873—Major Gibson; Ptes. J. Mitchell, Dow, C. Mitchell, Finlay, W. Street.
1874—Sgt. Hancock; Pte. Stone.
1875—Not any new seniors this year.
1876—Ptes. Etherington and J. McDonald.
1877—Pte. Geo. Margetts.
1878—Ptes. Miller and Kitto.
1879—Not any new seniors this year.
1880—Sgt. F. Lumsden; Ptes. Crawford and A. H. Young.
1881—Sgt. Geo. Murdoch; Ptes. W. N. Goodwin, James Omand.
1882—Sgt. H. Harvey; Corp. Madgett; Pte. H. Marris.
1883—S. Sgt. W. H. Clarke; Corpls. Woodward and Belau; Ptes. J. Peebles, D. Garson, Lipki, McRae, J. Harris, McArthur, McLeod, Forbes, Buglers Bull and Brown.
1884—Capt. W. G. Reid; Sgt. A. Bismarck; Ptes. Furmidge, Pecover, Kelk, A. Parkhill, J. Lawrence, F. Heath, Burniston, Keefer, Murray, Webb.
1885—Major McLaren; Lt. Tidswell; Col. Sgt. Miller; Ptes. A. Ray, Geo. Stiff, C. H. Smith, Lambert, P. Robertson, Th. Lawrence, Ely, Bettles, D. A. Walsh, Gilmer.
1886—Capt. E. Zealand; Col. Sgt. Harris; Corpls. T. Rattram. Meadows; Ptes. Smith, Hopper, Athawes, Best, Wigmore, G. Diamond, Chanter, Wilson, D. Henderson. A. Murdoch
1887—Col. Sgt. Stannard; Corp. Waddell; Ptes. C. Madgett, W. Wilson, J. Baker, Silk, T. Johns, A. Stewart, B. Clark, J. Clark, Ray.

1888—Col. Sgt. Grant; Sgts. C. Hamilton, F. Skedden; Corp. Martin; Ptes. M. Goodwin, Wible, Dixon, Robinson, Mepham, Reid, W. Southam, R. G. Freeborn, F. Rogers, W. Zimmerman, W. Haines. H. Richmond.
1889—Lt. Herring; Corp. Cline, Ptes. H. F. Beckett, R. Hooper, M. Skedden, E. B. Thomson, C. Zimmerman, E. J. Harris, Bugler W. McAndrew, Band'n T. H. King.
1890—Col. Sgt. J. Harvey; Corpls. S. A. Moore, Hopkins; Ptes. H. Barker, Addison, A. Stewart, Hampson, Gillespie, Lawson, Bugler W. W. Stewart, Band'n J. R. Burns.
1891—No record this year.
1892—Capt. Domville; Ptes. G. Ellicott, McGill, McKindsey, Pook, Turnbull, R. Miller, E. Reinholt, C. Dempster, Bugler A. Berryman, Band'n J. Divine.
1893—Capt. Moore; Sgt. Upsdell; Ptes. R. C. Allan, D. Gardner, Ogilvie, Jolley, C. N. Stewart, Band'n R. Magness, Bugler Heath.
1894—Sgt. A. Scott Ptes. J. R. Bates, G. Curran, T. LeMessurier, W. S. Millichamp, J. R. Miller, H. Bowstead, W. A. Wills, Dands'n R. Magness, Jr., Jas. Weedon.
1895—Sgt. J. A. Gibson; Ptes. C. McNab, D. Lambe, Bradshaw, W. Chiswell, F. Skedden, J. W. Aubrey, J. Kilgour, Band'n W, Robinson.
1896—Col. Sgt. Woodcroft; Ptes. E. D. Marshall, C. Cripps, H. Strickland, F. Blair, H. Walker, F. C. Chittenden, Dawe, Bugler McIntosh, Bandsman Rolls.
1897—Ptes. A. Porter, J. Rodgers, E. Fitzgerald, A. E. Cropper, N. Nudd, F. R. Findlay, J. Connon, Band'n W. Campbell, Bugler A. Hebner.
1898—Ptes. G. Bowman, F. F. Donohue, Adams, W. Drever, H. Stewart, Storms, L. Henning, F. W. Provost, W. Crawford, Bugler Spauls.

RECORD OF DISTRICT CHALLENGE CUP.

CONDITIONS.—To be competed for by three marksmen from any Volunteer Company in the Third Brigade Division, to be held in trust for the Association by Company making highest aggregate score.

Date of Match.	Rifle used.	No. shots	Ranges Yards.	COMPANY. Won by	Score.	Possible.	Date of Match.	Rifle used.	No. shots	Ranges Yards.	COMPANY Won by.	Score.	Possible.
			200, 400, 600.	Oakville.	54		Sep 30, Oct 1 &c	S. Enf'ld	1	200, 400, 600.	No. 2 Company 13th Bat.	109	135
			"	No. 1, 13th.	48		Oct. 5, 6, 82	"	1	"	No. 1, " "	101	135
			"	" 13th.	64		" 17, 18, 83	"	1	"	" A " "	103	135
			"	" 13th.	65		" 23, 24, 84	"	1	"	" K " "	104	135
Sept.	S. Enf'ld		"	" 13th.	52		" 19, 20, 85	"	1	"	" K " "	104	135
Aug.	"		"	" 13th.	25		Nov. 24, 25 86	"	1	"	" C " "	110	135
			"	No. 1, 13th. Waterdown	77	135	" 7, 8, 87	"	1	"	" C " "	93	135
			"	" 13th.	70	135	Oct. 22, 88	"	1	"	" C " "	109	135
Sep.			"	" 13th.		135	" 21, 22, 89	"	1	"	" A " "	101	135
Aug.			"	" 13th.		135	" 9, 10, 90	"	1	"	" E " "	105	135
Oct.			"	" 13th.	72	135	" 1, 2, 91	"	1	"	" C " "	108	135
Nov.			"	" 13th.	72	135	" 17, 18, 92	"	1	"	" C " "	107	135
Oct.			"	" 13th.	67	135	Sept. 21, 22, 93	"	1	"	" B " "	102	135
Sept.			"	" 13th.	61	135	Oct. 20, 21, 94	"	1	"	" C " "	117	135
Oct.			"	" 13th.	67	135	Nov. 22, 23, 95	"	1	"	" A " "	84	135
			"	" 13th.		135			1	"	" A " "		135
			"	No. 1, 13th.	71	135		L. En.	1	"	" A " 77th	123	135
			"	" 13th.	61	135	Nov.	"	1	"	" D " 13th	117	135

REMARKS.— At Grimsby 29th July to 4th August.
teams competed. Called Mrs. Gibson's Cup this year.
teams competed.
teams competed.
teams competed.

6 teams competed.
5 teams competed.
No competition owing to darkness.
Record score, shot at Dundas. (No 600 yards at V.R.C. ranges)
7 teams competed.

RECORD OF "OFFICERS'" CUP 13TH BATTALION INFANTRY.

CONDITIONS.—To be competed for annually by 12 men from each Company; to be won three times in succession for permanent possession by Company.

Date of Match.	Rifle used.	No. Shots	Ranges Yards.	COMPANY Won by.	Score.	Possible.	Date of Match.	Rifle used.	No. Shots	Ranges Yards.	COMPANY Won by.	Score.	Possible.
	Spencer			No. 1			Oct. 23, 24 74	Snider	5	600	No. E	171	600
Sept.	S. Enf			"			" 22, 23	"	5	"	" A	370	600
Aug.	S. Enf.			No competition			Nov. 24, 25 76	"	5	"	" A	122	600
				Waterdown Co. N.			Oct.	"	5	"	" C	364	600
Sept.	L. Snd'y			No. 1			"	"	5	"	" C	395	600
Aug.	"			"			"	"	5	"	" E	462	600
Oct.	"			"			"	"	5	"	" C	416	600
Nov.	"			"			"	"	5	"	" C	419	600
	"			4			"	"	5	"	" E	417	600
Sept.	"			"			Sept. 21, 22	"	7	300, 500, 600	" E	672	900
Oct.	Snider			" 4			Oct.	"	7	"	" A	963	1260
	"			" 2			Nov. 22, 23	"	7	"	" E	584	
	"			" 2				"	7	"	" A	724	
Sept. with Enf	"			" 2				"	7	"	" A	586	
Oct.	"			" 1			Nov. 8, 9	L. En.	7	"	" A	569	
	"			A					7				

REMARKS.— 1867, 1868, 1869.—For this period of three years conditions were 6 shots at 400, 500, 600 yards.
1870.—Won permanently by No. 1 Company.
1871.—No competition this year.
1880.—Won permanently by No. 2 Company.
1898.—Won permanently by A Company. 10 men only.

RECORD OF N. C. O. CUP 13TH BATTALION INFANTRY.

CONDITIONS.—To be competed for annually by 6 men from each Company; to be won four times in succession for permanent possession.

Date of Match.	Rifle used.	No. Shots	Ranges Yards.	COMPANY Won by.	Score.	Possible.	Date of Match.	Rifle used.	No. Shots	Ranges Yards.	COMPANY Won by.	Score.	Possible.
Oct. 17, 18 79	Snider	7	500, 600	No. 2	271	420	Oct. 9, 10 90	Snider	7	500, 600	No. C	297	420
" 19, 20 80	"	7	"	" 2	271	420	" 1, 2, 91	"	7	"	" C	277	420
Sep 28 Oct 2 81	"	7	"	" 2	291	420	" 17, 18 92	"	7	"	" C	299	420
Oct. 5, 6, 82	"	7	"	" D	301	420	Sept. 23, 24 93	"	7	"	" C	338	420
" 17, 18 83	"	7	"	" A	260	420	Oct. 20, 94	"	7	"	" K	337	420
" 20, 21 84	"	7	"	" A	270	420	Nov. 22, 95	"	7	"	" K	293	420
" 19, 20 85	"	7	"	" C	250	420		L. E.	7	"	" C	346	420
Nov. 24, 86	"	7	"	" C	239	420		"	7	300, 500	" A	307	420
" 7, 8, 87	"	7	"	" C	222	420	Nov. 5, 98	"	7	"			
Oct. 29, 30 88	"	7	"	" C	300	420			7				
" 21, 22 89	"	7	"	" C	327	420			7				

REMARKS.—1889—Won permanently by C Company. | 1895—Won permanently by C Company.

RECORD OF MERIDEN BRITTANIA CUP OR "JUNIOR CUP" 13TH BATTALION INFANTRY.

CONDITIONS.—Teams of four Junior Shots from each Company ; to be won twice in succession for permanent possession by one Company.

Date of Match.	Rifle used.	No. Shots	Ranges Yards.	COMPANY Won by.		Score.	Possible.	Date of Match.	Rifle used.	No. Shots	Ranges Yards.	COMPANY Won by.		Score.	Possible.
Oct. 20, 21 84	Snider	5	200, 400	No. E	...	121	200	Sep. 23, 29 91	Snider	5	200 400 500	No. A		218	
" 19, 20 85	"	5	"	" A	...	129	200	Oct. 23, 94	"	5	"	" E	...	721	
Nov. 24, 86	"	5	"	" A	...	181	200	Nov. 22, 91	"	5	"	" E	...	171	
" 7, 8, 87	"	5	"	" A	...	117	200			5	"	" A	...	216	
Oct. 29, 30 88	"	6	"	" F	...	477	900		I. E.	5	"	" A	...	207	
" 21, 22 89	"	5	"	" F	...	281	400	Nov. 5, 95	"	5	"	" F	...	272	
" 9, 10, 90	"	5	"	" E	...	241	400				1800				
" 1, 2, 91	"	5	"	" E	... no record						1901				
" 17, 18 92	"	5	"	" E	...	410	600								

REMARKS.—1886 This year 9 men, 20 rounds ; 5 each at 200, 300, 500, 400 yards. Won permanently by A Company.
1889—Won permanently by F Company.
1891—Won permanently by E Company.
1892—9 men, 10 shots each, 200, 400, 500 yards.
1895—Won permanently by E Company.
1897 Won permanently by A Company.

13TH BATTALION RECORD AT DOMINION RIFLE ASSOCIATION MATCHES, OTTAWA, UP TO AND INCLUDING 1899.

The MacDougall, won by Pte. D. Mitchell 1873 ; Sergt. D. Mitchell 1875 ; Sergt. T. Mitchell 1876 ; Col.-Sergt. E. Skedden 1896.
Caron, won by Thirteenth Battalion Infantry 1844 and 1847.
British Challenge Shield, won by Thirteenth Battalion Infantry 1885.
Lansdowne Challenge Cup, won by Thirteenth Battalion Infantry 1889, 1891 and 1897.
Walker Cup, won by Thirteenth Battalion Infantry 1896 and 1897.

Patterson Cup, won by Col.-Sergt. E. Skedden 1897.
Davis & Sons' Cup, won by Thirteenth Battalion Infantry 1897. (Record Score) and 1897.
Gillespie Challenge Cup, won by Thirteenth Battalion Infantry 1897.
Governor General's Gold Medal, (first time) won by Col.-Sergt. E. Skedden 1896.

13TH BATTALION RECORD AT ONTARIO RIFLE ASSOCIATION MATCHES, TORONTO, UP TO AND INCLUDING 1899.

N. R. Association Medals, won by Corp. T. Mitchell 1876 ; Sergt. D. Mitchell 1877 ; Lieut.-Col. Gibson 1890 ; S. Sergt. Geo. Margetts 1883 and 1884 ; Sergt. H. Marris 1890 ; Lieut. W. L. Ross 1897.

D. R. A. Medals, won by Sergt. D. Mitchell, silver, 1877 ; Sergt. D. Mitchell, silver, 1891 ; Pte. T. H. Hayhurst, G. M., bronze, 1895 ; Corp. G. W. Spencer, bronze, 1896.

Gov. General's Medals, won by Sergt. D. Mitchell, silver, 1870 ; Pte. J. Mitchell, bronze, 1870 ; Pte. W. Mitchell, silver, 1873 ; Sergt. D. Mitchell, bronze, 1880 ; Pte. H. Marris, silver, 1882 ; Capt. E. G. Zealand, bronze, 1886 ; Sergt. H. Marris, bronze, 1891 ; Sergt. D. Mitchell, silver, 1893 ; Lieut. A. Pain, bronze, 1893 ; Sergt. D. Mitchell, silver, 1896.

Ladies' Challenge Cup, won by Thirteenth Battalion Infantry 1873, 1877, 1880 and 1882.
Tait Cup, won by Thirteenth Battalion Infantry 1876, 1878, 1879, 1880, 1886, 1891, 1897 and 1899.

Brassey Company Cup, won in 1874 by No. 1 Co'y Thirteenth Infantry ; in 1876 by No. A Co'y ; in 1877 by No. 1 Co'y ; in 1878 by No. 1 Co'y ; in 1881 by No. A Co'y ; in 1891 by No. C Co'y ; in 1897 by No. F Co'y.

Merchants' Cup, won by Thirteenth Battalion Infantry 1872, 1874, 1876, 1877, 1879 and 1880. Won permanently by Thirteenth Battalion in 1880.

Gzowski (Skirmishing) Cup, won by Thirteenth Battalion Infantry 1893.

Canadian Club Jubilee Challenge Trophy, won by 13th Battalion Infantry 1898 and 1899.

O. R. Ass'n Aggregate Cup, won by Major J. M. Gibson 1873 and 1874. (The Dartnell Cup for Snider Aggregate).

Elkington Cup, for the highest individual aggregate score, 1870, Sergt. D. Mitchell ; 1873, Pte. H. Marris ; 1877, Corp. H. Marris ; 1880, Sergt. W. M. Goodwin ; 1891, S. Sergt. D. Mitchell ; 1897, Lieut. W. L. Ross.

REPRESENTATIVES OF THE 13TH BATTALION INFANTRY ON WIMBLEDON AND BISLEY TEAMS.

1871, Ontario Team—Col. Skinner, Thirteenth Battalion, Commandant. Members, Col.-Sergt. Robt. Omand, Sergt. F. Sache, Lieut. J. Little, Pte. Jos Mason, Pte. Geo. Murison.
1872, Dominion Teams—Capt. James Adam, Col.-Sergt. Robert Omand.
1873.* Col.-Sergt. Robt. Omand, Pte John Mitchell.
1874, Major J. M. Gibson, Capt. J. J. Mason, Col.-Sergt. Robert Omand, Corp. A. Pain, *Pte. T. Mitchell.
1875, Major J. M. Gibson,
1876, *Sergt. D. Mitchell, *Sergt. T. Mitchell.
1877, *Sergt. D. Mitchell, Sergt. John Mitchell, *Sergt. Thos. Mitchell.
1878, None.
1879, *Lieut.-Col. Gibson, Capt. Jas. Adam, Pte. H. Marris, Pte. John Mitchell, Pte. Thos. Mitchell.
1880, None.
1881, Sergt. A. Pain, Col.-Sergt. O. Hancock, Sergt. D. Mitchell, *Pte. H. Marris, Pte. Jos, Mason, Lieut.-Col. J. M. Gibson, Commandant.
1882, None.
1883, Staff Sergt. F. B. Ross.
1884, Staff-Sergt. Geo. T. Margetts, *Pte. John Mitchell, Corp. W. M. Goodwin,
1885, *Pte. H. Marris.
1886, Capt. James Adam.

1887, *Corp. H. Marris, Pte. H. Graham.
1888, Capt. E. G. Zealand,
1889, None.
1890, None ; new team at Bisley.
1890, Capt, E. G. Zealand, Capt. F. B. Ross, *Sergt. H. Marris.
1891, Sergt. H. Marris.
1892, *Sergt. H. Marris, *Staff-Sergt. D. Mitchell.
1893, None.
1894, Staff-Sergt. D. Mitchell, Pte. T. H Hayhurst, Lieut, W. L. Ross.
1895, Col.-Sergt. E. Skedden, Sergt. H. Marris, *Pte. T. H. Hayhurst.
1896, *Lt. W. L. Ross, *Staff-Sgt. T. H. Hayhurst, G. M., Sgt. Major S. J. Huggins, Sgt. T. Mitchell.
1897, Major J. J. Mason, Commandant ; *Lt. W. L. Ross, Col.-Sgt. E. Skedden, Sgt. H. Garson.
1898, Lieut. A. Pain, Lieut. W. L. Ross, Staff-Sgt. T. H. Hayhurst, Sgt. C. W. Spencer.
1899, Major F. B. Ross, Lieut. R. A. Robertson, Sergt.-Major S. J. Huggins.

NOTE.—Those marked * members of Kolapore Eight.
In 1879 Col. Gibson won Prince of Wales Prize, 94 out of 105, Snider B. L., record score ; 1895 Col.-Sgt. Skedden won Daily Graphic Cup after record for tie shooting ; 1895 Pte. T. H. Hayhurst won Queen's Prize after tie shooting.

87

RECORD OF "LAWYERS'" CUP.

CONDITIONS.—1 Officer, 1 Sergeant, 1 Corporal and 5 Privates from any one Company to compose the team; the first Company winning it three times to own it.

Date of Match.	Rifle used.	No. Shots	Ranges Yards.	COMPANY Won by.	Score.	Possible.	Date of Match.	Rifle used.	No. Shots	Ranges Yards.	COMPANY Won by.	Score.	Possible.
		Spencer	4 400, 600	No. 1	102	120	Nov. 21, 1875	L. Bni.	5 400, 600	No. 1	... ...	324	480
Sept.		N. Enf.	5 "	" 1	177	480	" 17, 76	"	5 "	" 2	406	600
Aug. 4		"	5 "	2, Waterdown	114	480	Sept. 6, 7, 77	"	5 "	" 1	443	600
		"	5 "	" 2 ...	221	480	Oct. 14, 15, 78	Snider	5 "	" 1	437	600
		"	5 "	" 2	117	480	" 19, 20, 80	"	5 "	" 4	402	600
Sept.		L. Sni.	5 "	" 2 ...	142	480	" 19, 20, 80	"	5 "	" 1	471	600
Aug.		"	5 "	" 2	101	600	Sept. 9, and						
Oct.		"	5 "	" 2	101	400	Oct. 1, 81	"	5 "	" 2	438	600

REMARKS.—... Only 200 and 400 yards this year.
... 1871, 1872 Won permanently by No. 2 Company.
... 1 men from each Company.

1874—7 men from each Company.
1875—8 men from each Company.
1876—10 men from each Company and won permanently by No. 2.

RECORD OF "IRISH PROTESTANT BENEVOLENT SOCIETY" CUP.

CONDITIONS. Teams of 5 men from each Company; to be won twice in succession for permanent possession.

Date of Match.	Rifle used.	No. Shots	Ranges Yards.	COMPANY Won by.	Score.	Possible.	Date of Match.	Rifle used.	No. Shots	Ranges Yards.	COMPANY Won by.	Score.	Possible.
Aug. 26,	N. E.	5 400, 500	No. 2			142	200	Sept. 9, 10, 72	S. E.	5 400, 500	No. 1	...	148	200
	"	5 "	" 1			118	200							

REMARKS. 1872 Won permanently by No. 1 Company.

RECORD OF "PIERCE" CUP.

CONDITIONS. Teams of 5 men from each Company; to be won three times for permanent possession

Date of Match.	Rifle used.	No. Shots	Ranges Yards.	COMPANY Won by.	Score.	Possible.	Date of Match.	Rifle used.	No. Shots	Ranges Yards.	COMPANY Won by.	Score.	Possible.
Oct. 2, 17, 74	L. Sni.	5 400, 600	No. 1		151	200	Nov. 17, 76	L. Bni.	5 400, 500	No. 2	188	250
Nov. 22, 75	"	5 "	" 1 ...	157	200	Sept. 6, 7, 77	"	5 "	" 1	176	250

REMARKS. 1877—Won permanently by No. 1 Company.

RECORD OF "LIEUT. ADAMS" CUP.

CONDITIONS—Teams of 6 men.

Date of Match.	Rifle used.	No. Shots	Ranges Yards.	COMPANY Won by.	Score.	Possible.	Date of Match.	Rifle used.	No. Shots	Ranges Yards.	COMPANY Won by.	Score.	Possible.
Oct. 17, 18 79 " 19, 20, 80	Snider "	400, 500, 600	No. 2	...	275	450	Sept. 30 and Oct. 3, 81	Snider	200, 500, 600	No. 2	...	269	450

REMARKS.—1880—No match for this cup this year.

RECORD OF "MRS. J. M. GIBSON'S" CUP.

Date of Match.	Rifle used.	No. Shots	Ranges Yards.	COMPANY Won by.	Score.	Possible.	Date of Match.	Rifle used.	No. Shots	Ranges Yards.	COMPANY Won by.	Score.	Possible.
Oct. 5, 6, 82 " 17, 18 83	Snider "	200, 500, 600	No. A " D	... ...	274 303	450 450	Oct. 20, 21, 84 " 19, 20, 85	Snider "	200, 500, 600	No. E " E	... ...	308 287	450 450

www.ingramcontent.com/pod-product-compliance
Lightning Source LLC
Chambersburg PA
CBHW020327090426
42735CB00009B/1439